Lautréamont

KENNIKAT PRESS

NATIONAL UNIVERSITY PUBLICATIONS

SERIES ON LITERARY CRITICISM

General Editor

EUGENE GOODHEART

Professor of Literature, Massachusetts Institute of Technology

PAUL ZWEIG

LAUTRÉAMONT

The Violent Narcissus

NATIONAL UNIVERSITY PUBLICATIONS
KENNIKAT PRESS
Port Washington, N.Y./London/1972

The section "The Violent Narcissus" is a substantially revised version, in
English translation by the author, of *Lautréamont ou les violences du
Narcisse*. Paris, Lettres Modernes Minard, 1967. (Archives des lettres
Modernes, No. 74), and is here published with the permission of M. J.
Minard, Paris.

Library of Congress Catalog Card No: 78-189562
ISBN: 0-8046-9021-9

Manufactured in the United States of America

Published by
Kennikat Press, Inc.
Port Washington, N.Y./London

To My Mother and Father

TABLE OF CONTENTS

Preface

Although Lautréamont's fame has grown steadily in France since his discovery by surrealists almost fifty years ago, his work remains relatively unknown in America. This is unfortunate, for he is surely one of the most unusual figures in nineteenth-century French literature, considered by many to be the equal of more celebrated poets like Nerval, Baudelaire and Rimbaud.

My aim in writing the present volume has been to familiarize the reader with the work of this underrated poet.

I have divided my study into three parts. The first is essentially introductory. It describes the traditions upon which Lautréamont drew in creating his masterpiece, *Les Chants de Maldoror*. It evokes the contemporaneity of the poem's peculiar vision, and attempts to give an idea of the tantalizing mysteries which continue to surround Lautréamont's life. The second part was originally written and published in French, some years ago. It has been substantially revised into its present form and presents a meditation upon themes which govern the unity of *Les Chants de Maldoror*. In the third part, I have attempted to correct what I am convinced is an essential lack, by translating a number of passages from *Maldoror* into the sort of lively English which the poem deserves.

Paul Zweig

New York, 1972

Lautréamont

PART ONE:
Lautréamont
and the Poetry of Evil

I

Les Chants de Maldoror[1] is undoubtedly the masterpiece of nineteenth-century satanism. The poem's savagery and dark humor have rarely been equaled in literature. Lautréamont's hero, Maldoror, is a terrifying yet strangely comic figure, as when he transforms himself into a giant squid fastening his suckers in the Creator's armpit, or leaps headfirst into the ocean to copulate with his "living portrait," a female shark. Rarely has poetry expressed such a mood of demonic revolt.

The originality of *Maldoror* does not lie only in its subject matter, of course. Since the *petit romantisme* of Petrus Borel and Aloysius Bertrand in the 1830s, a current of somber hallucinatory poetry had taken over the foreground of French literature, in Gérard de Nerval's hermetic sonnets and his dream epic, *Aurélia*; in Baudelaire's *Fleurs du Mal*, and Charles Nodier's tales; also in the vast wave of popular literature represented by the *roman noir*.[2]

[1] Referred to henceforth as *Maldoror.*

[2] *The Mysteries of Paris* and *The Wandering Jew*, by Eugene Sue; *Rocombole*, by Ponson du Terreil; and *The Memoirs of the Devil*, by Frederick Soulie are among the best known examples.

By the time Isidore Ducasse published the First Canto of *Maldoror*, in 1866, the subject matter of evil and revolt had been formulated into a convention upon which the poet could draw not only for the orientation of his poem, but also for his literary pseudonym. The name, the Count of Lautréamont, is adapted from the hero of Eugene Sue's feuilleton novel, *Latréaumont*, which was first published in 1838. Sue's character has a flavor of the diabolical which must have appealed to Isidore Ducasse:

> Courageous to the point of foolhardiness, with a health of steel; so frighteningly strong that it was said he could lift up a horse on his wide shoulders, or knock it down with a blow of his enormous fist; extremely skilled in all the exercises of body and mind, fearing neither God nor man, capable of undertaking anything, he became incredibly stubborn and willful when it was a question of satisfying his unbridled passions.[3]

Sue's Latréaumont, like Melmoth, or the Monk, or Balzac's Vautrin, is an extravagant presence for whom evil and energy are synonymous. Because energy, like fire, destroys limits, such characters embody a destructive radiance which defines the genre of the *roman noir* and the Gothic novel, telling them apart from the high traditions of the novel itself.

Novelists like Thackeray or Jane Austen, or Balzac himself (in most of *The Human Comedy*), describe and celebrate the pattern of "realities" which compose a life. They present us with unique characters playing out their lives in equally unique social circumstances. In the *roman noir*, on the other hand, it is not the pattern which is celebrated, not the "realistic," highly articulated history, but the energies which disrupt the history. The hero of the *roman noir*, and of the Gothic novel before it, is perverse and essentially mysterious; he is a character whose allegiance to himself is so compelling that he refuses to be imprisoned by the limits of circumstance and society, by the prison of the ordinary to which novels are committed. Such heroes are "evil" because they come from elsewhere, like falling stars, or like devils. They are criminals (Rocombole and Vautrin), or condemned exiles

[3] François Caradec, *Isidore Ducasse, Comte de Lautréamont*, La Table Ronde, Paris, 1970, quoted on p. 187.

(Melmoth); they are solitary characters whose consolations lie not in companionship and society, but in the demonstration of their own compelling vitality. They are also victims, men of *ressentiment*, and therefore every impulse of their character is an act of revenge upon the society to which they cannot belong and refuse to belong.

In this sense, the *roman noir* and the Gothic novel are anti-novels. And the rebellious mood of the late French Romantics grows out of this tradition of avenging energies. There is a somber Rousseauism in Nerval, Baudelaire, Lautréamont and Rimbaud. "Man was born free but everywhere he is in chains."[4] To undo the chains, these men chose to undo the pattern of society in their own psyches. This is the impetus of Rimbaud's drug experiments, his "reasoned unreasoning of the senses," of Nerval's fascination with the archaic freedom of dream images. And this is the commitment Isidore Ducasse expresses in a letter to his publisher a year before his death: "I have celebrated evil, as Mickiewitz, Byron, Milton, Southey, Alfred de Musset, Baudelaire, etc., did before me. Naturally I exaggerated the tone a little, to create something new in the mode of that sublime literature. . . ." (398)[5] Ducasse's declaration of intention echoes the disingenuousness of his immediate ancestor, Baudelaire, who wrote of his *Fleurs du Mal*, "Since famous poets have long since staked out the more flowery realms of poetic subject matter, I thought it would be interesting . . . to extract beauty out of evil." The innocuous "literary" tone of Lautréamont's letter points to an ambivalence in *Maldoror* which one finds equally in the whole tradition he identifies himself with. On the one hand, in writing his poem he embraced a cultural form, a convention for which his rhetorical gifts were uniquely fitted. What he is doing is "literary." Like Baudelaire, and his other avowed masters, he has chosen among subject matters. But the genre he has chosen mines a dangerous territory of inward sentiments, it

[4] Jean Jacques Rousseau *Le Contrat Social*.

[5] All page references, unless otherwise indicated, correspond to Lautréamont's *Oeuvres Complètes*, Jose Corti, Paris, 1969. Translations into English are by the author.

draws upon images, energies, and emotions which are blind and unsocializable. That is why they attract him. They express an impregnable "freedom" which the poet experiences in his own psyche: freedom from morality and authority; freedom from society; eventually, in *Maldoror*, freedom from the confinement of the human form itself. To fulfil his "literary" commitment, and dramatize the animus of revolt and *ressentiment* which the genre demands, the poet must walk a tightrope into the archaic revolts of his psyche, closer than one perhaps should ever be to the permanent insanity which lies beneath the outer walls of personality. At the end of his Second Canto, Lautréamont exclaims:

> No . . . don't let that haggard pack of diggers and shovels come deeper through the land mines of this impious song! The crocodile won't change a word of the vomit pouring from the inside his skull. Too bad if some furtive shadow, excited by the worthy goal of avenging human-ity, which has been unjustly attacked by me, should slide open the door of my room, brushing along the wall like a seagull's wing, to plunge a knife through the ribs of the scavenger of celestial wrecks! The clay might as well dissolve its atoms this way as any other. (219)

Apparently Lautréamont understood the danger of his poem, and was fascinated by it. The starkness and the strange immediacy of the language here characterize *Maldoror*. The entire poem seems to take place at an intersection between literature and madness. The language is warped into uniqueness by the associative pres-sures of the primitive mind (the unconscious), and yet con-trolled, magnificently, by the rhetorical form of which the poet never loses sight. The result makes the poem seem self-generating and monolithic. One experiences *Maldoror* as a unique vision of cruelty and revolt, a poem whose rhythm is so compelling that it must be "authentic," a true if terrifying cry from the depths.

This undoubtedly explains the reverence for Lautréamont ex-pressed by André Breton, and the French surrealists, who insisted that *Maldoror* must never be allowed to enter literary history, inserted between "this fellow and that fellow"; that Lautréamont had, at all costs, to be rescued from "literature." It also explains the feeling of scandal created when large passages in *Maldoror* were found to have been cribbed word for word from naturalist encyclopedias, and others were shown to echo, in a style just short of plagiarism, a whole panoply of popular writers from Michelet and Victor Hugo, to Goethe, Byron, Baudelaire, Sue, Shakespeare and others, too. In fact, on the evidence, few works of literature in the nineteenth century (which was so compelled by the romantic values of "authenticity" and "sincerity") were as resolutely literary as Lautréamont's late Gothic epic.

Ultimately, the fascination *Maldoror* continues to exert on readers probably will be defined by this enigma of a poem which breathes a uniqueness that is all but hallucinatory, while clinging at every moment to all its cultural and literary origins. In the end, one cannot decide whether Isidore Ducasse was a master of rhetorical effects, and a very great master at that, or a man driven mad by writing, whose poem must be read as a history of his madness.

What is one to make, for example, of passages like the following:

> The brother of the leech walked slowly in the forest. Several times he stops, opening his mouth to speak. But each time his throat contorts, refusing to release the aborted effort. At last he cries out: O Man, when you see a dead dog on its back, wedged into a lock so that it can't float away, don't act like everyone else and pick the worms out of its swollen stomach with your hands, contemplate them wonderingly, open a knife, and then cut up a number of them, saying to yourself, you too will be just like that dog. What mystery are you searching for? Not me, or the four webbed claws of the sea-bear of the Boreal ocean, have been able to discover the problem of life. Beware, night approaches, and you've been here since morning. What will your family and your little sister say when they see you coming home so late? Wash your hands, take the road that goes to where you sleep. . . . What's that creature down there, on the horizon, who dares to approach me fearlessly, with oblique, tormented leaps? What majesty, mixed with serene sweetness! Its gaze is deep, although it is tender. Its enormous eyelids flap in the breeze, and seem to be alive. It is unknown to me. When I look into its monstrous eyes my body trembles for the first time since I sucked the dry tits of what they call a mother. A halo of blinding light surrounds him. When he has spoken, everything in nature becomes quiet, and shudders. Since you want to come to me, as if drawn by a magnet, I won't stop you. How beautiful he is! It hurts me to say it. You must be strong, because your face is more than human, sad as the universe, beautiful as suicide. I abhor you with all my might,

and would rather see a snake wound around my neck from the beginning of time, than your eyes. . . .What! It's you, toad! . . . fat toad!
. . . unfortunate toad. . . .Pardon! . . . Pardon! . . . What are you doing
on this earth of the damned? But what have you done to your viscous
and fetid warts, to seem so lovely? (157-8)

In a moment of madness, I could take you by the arms and twist them
like a wash that you wring dry, or break them with a snap, like two dry
branches, and then use force to make you eat them. Taking your head
in my hands, sweetly and caressingly, I could press my avid fingers into
the lobes of your innocent brain, with a smile on my lips, extracting a
usable fat to wash my eyes, which hurt with life's eternal insomnia.
Sewing your eyelids together with a needle, I could shut out the
spectacle of the universe, making it impossible for you to find your
way; I wouldn't be the one to guide you. Lifting up your virgin body
with an arm of steel, I could seize you by the legs and roll you around
me like a slingshot, concentrating my forces on the last circumference,
as I heave you against a wall. Each drop of blood will stain a human
breast, and frighten men, placing them before an example of my evil
deeds! . . . Don't worry, I'll order half a dozen of my servants to guard
the venerated remains of your body, and keep them from the hunger of
wild dogs. The body is probably stuck to the wall like a ripe pear, and
hasn't fallen to earth; but dogs can make high leaps, if you don't watch
out. (173)

The language is taut and controlled. The images never seem
stereotyped or compulsive. On the contrary, the aura of dream-
like surprise in the first passage, the sadistic violence in the
second, are positively sharpened by a fine line of humor which
creates the impression of artistic control in the midst of frenzy.
Or is the impression we get rather one of psychotic detachment,
resulting from the emotional disassociation of the illness, as the
psychiatrist Jean-Pierre Soulier argues in his study *Lautréamont:
Génie ou Maladie Mentale?*[6]

The debate concerning Lautréamont's sanity is an old one.
Léon Bloy, who came across an old copy of *Maldoror* in the
1880s, was the first to make the judgment that "this is a madman
speaking, the most deplorable, most painful of madmen." Since
then, virtually every critic from Remy de Gourmont to Maurice
Blanchot has felt obliged to reinterpret the evidence and decide
for or against, sane or not sane. The arguments have all had a

[6] Droz, Geneva, 1964.

single deficiency. Virtually nothing is known of Isidore Ducasse, aside from the barest outlines of his life, a few letters, and a sample of his handwriting. The only evidence is *Maldoror*, and there a problem arises. The partisans of sanity and genius point to the exquisite artistic control which virtually never lapses in the poem, and decide that such a coherence is proof that the author was sane. But they are answered quite professionally that a whole category of mental illness, which used to be called *folie raisonante* or *délire d'interpretation* ("reasoning madness," "delirium of interpretation") and is now called schizophrenia or paranoia, can manifest itself precisely in such a sustained, gloriously flawless system of language, that loss of control need have nothing to do with psychosis until a very advanced stage. In such cases the control in psychosis is strangely misapplied, creating a world of coherent but exaggeratedly idiosyncratic, and even archaic images.

Into this argument, which probably will never be resolved, another note must be injected. At some point in the nineteenth century, madness became an interesting subject matter for poets and novelists. It became worthwhile, for literary and cultural reasons, to learn how to imitate the style and the insights of madmen. One thinks of Gogol's *Diary of a Madman*, Dostoyevsky's *Notes From the Underground*, Nerval's *Aurélia*. There are long passages in *Melmoth*, where Maturin describes the effects of madness, and gives his version of the kind of hallucinatory talk that goes on in an insane asylum, apparently because he thought it would interest (and not disgust) his readers. As a matter of fact, the fascination with insanity has become a kind of orthodoxy in modern culture. We enjoy paintings by schizophrenics and are thrilled by the strange, sometimes pathetic connections they can make between words.[7] Not only that, but the conventions established in much modernist literature are derived from versions of madness, usually psychosis. One thinks of the stereotyped dialogue in Ionesco's plays, of the claustrophobic empti-

---

[7] I still remember a phrase recorded in a mental hospital which, to me, has the eeriness of a great short poem: *"la terre bouge; elle ne m'inspire aucune confiance."* "The earth moves; it inspires me with no confidence."

ness in Beckett's work, of Marcel's neurasthenia in *A la Recherche du Temps Perdu*, or of Benjy's idiot monologue in *The Sound and the Fury*.

The insight expressed by this fascination with madness can, perhaps, be described as follows. We are enclosed by a civilization which has become increasingly deadly. The behavior that civilization teaches us to assume is often dangerous to ourselves and to others. The definition of sanity and responsibility which it wants us to believe in is, in fact, simply mad. In such a case, it may be that madmen are the only true sane men.

In other words it has become a perfectly sane artistic choice to imitate in literature the procedures of psychotic thought. But what happens if the imitation is too good? Can the poet's work be taken as evidence that he has crossed over to the other side? What happens if the poet's choice of literary mode coincides all too well with an impulse in his character, so that, by playing with the metaphor of psychotic language, he weakens the controls in his own personality? There is another sort of question, too. Isn't it possible for the poet to exorcise his personal demons in the cathartic work of the writing itself, to stay sane because his psychotic dispositions have been transposed into a language which others will value and understand? The examples of Strindberg and of William Blake come to mind.

These are questions worth raising. But the case of Lautréamont reminds us how circumspect one must be in attempting to resolve any of them as long as one's only evidence is the literature itself.

In any case, the immediacy of Lautréamont's rhetoric in *Maldoror*, the almost hypnotic urgency of the images, mingled with humor of the strangest kind, make the poem seem absolutely contemporary. Obviously the model of mad freedom which Lautréamont proposes has lost none of its power. In fact, a great deal of recent drug literature exploits an identical commitment to "mind-blowing" liberation. One thinks of William Burroughs' *Naked Lunch* and *Nova Express*, or of Carlos Castañeda's *Teachings of Don Juan*, where the hallucinations induced by mescal have a quality of deadly adventure which recalls

Maldoror. Isidore Ducasse may or may not have written his epic under the pressure of encroaching psychosis; but *Maldoror* is, by its own frequent admission, a book of the mad, whose half-humorous intention is to liberate the reader into madness.

Throughout the poem Lautréamont toys with the suggestion of his own insanity, accusing the All-Powerful of having placed his "soul between the boundaries of madness, and those furious thoughts which kill more slowly...." (164) At one point he describes a striking scene in which Maldoror is haunted by a spectre, as in the spookiest of Gothic novels:

> what shadow casts the image of its shriveled silhouette upon my wall with such incredible power.... A flock of hungry birds hover near your face; they love meat that doesn't belong to them, and defend the usefulness of pursuit, beautiful as skeletons plucking leaves of the panoccos in Arkansas.... But maybe you don't have a face; your shadow walks on the wall in a feverish shake of human vertebrae, like the deformed symbol of a ghostly dance. (267)

The episode builds in a crescendo of grotesque imagery, until at last Maldoror is forced to recognize the phantom which has been haunting him:

> There's only one thing left to do: break this mirror into pieces with the help of a stone.... It's not the first time the nightmare of the momentary loss of memory has set up residence in my imagination, when, by inflexible optic laws, I have been confronted with the ignorance of my own image. (271)

Such hints of mental disassociation become more frequent and more elaborate in the poem as Lautréamont develops the conception of his liberating insanity, which is like an expedition into some exotic domain where all identities, all forms have become unstable. "It is a man, or a stone, or a tree that will begin the Fourth Canto.... In the middle as at the beginning of life angels stay the same; how long is it since I stopped resembling myself?" (250)

Then at last, after the reader has been cajoled, dazzled, chilled, and yet compelled too, by the satanic transformation which *Maldoror* has enacted before his eyes, Lautréamont turns to him in a passage of double talk, mingled with startling argument:

> My friend, isn't it true that, to a certain extent, my poem has won you
> over? Then what keeps you from going the rest of the way? The limit
> between your taste and mine is invisible; you'll never really understand
> it; proof that the limit itself doesn't exist. In which case, consider this
> (I only touch on the question here): it may not be impossible that
> you've signed a treaty of alliance with obstination, agreeable daughter
> of the mule, copious spring of intolerance. If I didn't know that you
> weren't stupid, I wouldn't complain about this. There is no need for
> you to get stuck in the membraned carapace of an axiom you think is
> unshakeable. Other axioms are unshakeable too, and they advance
> parallel to yours. If you have a strong preference for caramel (that
> admirable farce of nature), no one will think it's a crime; but someone
> whose intelligence is more active and capable of greater things, may
> prefer arsenic and pepper, and have good reasons to do so, without
> meaning to impose their peaceful domination over those who tremble
> with fear before a shrew-mouse, or the talking expression of the
> surfaces of a cube. (286)

The effect of the passage is comic, and yet convincing in its way.
Only by loosening his grip on the forms of his own sanity, can
the reader demonstrate true broadness of mind. Otherwise he will
remain locked in the axioms of reason as in a prison, and will
never understand the enjoyment he has hypocritically taken in
the "mind-blowing" episodes of *Maldoror*. Besides, the reader
had better be careful, because at that very moment "new thrills
are appearing in the intellectual atmosphere," and what better
way could there be to meet them than to plunge, cathartically,
into the bath of *Maldoror*'s insane vision.

Isidore Ducasse would have been surprised by the accuracy of
his prophecy. A year or two later Rimbaud appeared on the
literary scene, occupying precisely the place Isidore Ducasse had
designated for him. Maldoror turns out to have been a kind of
John the Baptist. But Ducasse was dead by the time the new
literature erupted. One of the few indisputable facts in the
biography of Isidore Ducasse is his death, November 24, 1870, at
the age of twenty-four, a year before Rimbaud came to Paris, on
the eve of the Commune, perhaps at the very moment the *Bateau
Ivre* was being written.

Lautréamont rarely leaves his reader with the comfort of an
abstract formulation. He concludes the above "therapeutic" ex-
hortations with a course of practical advice that seals the argu-

ment once and for all. Rarely have the tools of discourse been used for such manipulative and ultimately grotesque ends:

> Believe me, in all things habit is necessary; and since the instinctive disgust which you felt when you first began reading, has notably diminished, in inverse proportion to the pages you've turned, like a large boil which has been lanced, there is hope, although your head is still sick, that your cure will quickly reach its final period. In my opinion, it's obvious that you're in full convalescence; although your face is thin, alas! But.. ... have courage! You have an unusual mind, I love you, and haven't given up hope of your complete deliverance, as long as you take a few medicinal ingredients, which I'm sure will hasten the final disappearance of all your symptoms. For an astringent and tonic nourishment, first of all, you will tear off your mother's arms (if she's still alive), cut them into small pieces and eat them, in a single day, without betraying the trace of an emotion on your face. If your mother is too old, take another surgical specimen, a younger and fresher one, whose flesh is more easily scraped, and whose tarsal bone, when she walks, finds good support to balance forward: your sister, for example. . . . The most lenitive mixture I advise is a basin full of pitted blenoragic pus in which has been dissolved beforehand a pilous cyst of the ovary, a follicular chancre, an inflamed foreskin peeled back from the glans by a paraphymosis, and three red slugs. If you follow my prescription, my poetry will receive you with open arms, like a louse severing the root of a hair with its kisses. (288)

The violence of *Maldoror* is committed to a kind of ironic pedagogy. The poem's satanic vision, we are told mockingly, is indeed therapeutic. It is meant to cure the reader of what Mathurin (one of Lautréamont's favorite writers), called "the curse of sanity."[8]

---

[8] *Melmoth*, University of Nebraska Press, Lincoln, 1961, p. 34.

II

Although the subject matter of *Maldoror* belongs to a tradition of romantic revolt, the poem is profoundly original in its use of language, mingling elaborate rhetorical periods with images of the most singular nature, as in the famous series of comparatives which Lautréamont develops in the final portion of the poem. André Breton was quick to recognize the "surreality" of passages like these which now and again interrupt and modify the narrative:

> The scarabee disappeared over the horizon, beautiful as the trembling of the hands in alcoholism. (294)

> The great vulture, beautiful as the law of arrested development of the chest in adults whose growth is not proportionate to the quantity of molecules their organism assimilates, vanished in the upper layers of the atmosphere. (294)

> Although his face was not human, he seemed beautiful to me as the two long tentacular-shaped filaments of an insect; or else, like a precipitated funeral; or else, like the law governing the reconstitution of mutilated organs; and, above all, like an excessively putrefying liquid. (291)

The most famous of these *beau comme* ("beautiful as") passages became a surrealist watchword in the 1920s. It describes Mervyn,

a beautiful blond English boy, who is Maldoror's principal victim
in the final Canto:

> He is beautiful as the retractability of the claws in birds of prey; or else,
> like the uncertainty of muscular movements in wounds of the soft parts
> of the posterior cervical region; or else, like a perpetual rat trap which is
> always reset by the animal it catches, enabling it alone to catch rats
> indefinitely, and to function even when it is hidden under straw; and
> above all, like the fortuitous encounter on a dissecting table between an
> umbrella and a sewing machine. (327)

There is a spirit of surreal buffoonery in passages like these which
convinced Breton that Lautréamont was the historical master of
humour noir ("black humor") and a model for the liberating
pranksterism which Dada and the surrealists felt to be one of
their anticultural duties.

Without the fanatical interest shown in *Maldoror* by the surrealist group, it is doubtful that Lautréamont's work would have
attracted the attention it finally has. *Maldoror* was unkown and
practically unpublished until the 1890s, twenty years after the
death of Isidore Ducasse. At that time, a publisher, Louis Genonceaux, followed up a rumor he had heard about an unusual prose
poem written by a completely unknown poet who had been dead
for a long time. It turned out that the poem, *Les Chants de
Maldoror*, had been contracted for by the publisher Albert Lacroix in the late 1860s, but that the publication itself never had
come about. Perhaps Lacroix backed out because of the poem's
blasphemous violence; or perhaps Ducasse never finished paying
out the costs (since the contract called for payment by the
author). Of that proposed edition only ten copies were bound
and sent to Ducasse, who had little time to enjoy or publicize
them, since he died of mysterious causes shortly afterward.

In 1874 the Belgian publisher Verboeckhoven, who had been
an associate of Lacroix's and had inherited the printed but
unbound copies when Lacroix went bankrupt, decided to recoup
some of his investment. He had *Maldoror* bound and sold in
Belgium by the firm of Rozez. It was the first real edition of the
whole poem, and it went completely unnoticed, though copies of
the Belgian edition could apparently still be found in bookstalls
in the early 1900s.

Genonceaux's 1890 edition did attract some notice. The French critic Remy de Gourmont wrote a piece on *Maldoror* in the *Mercure* in 1891, and his article probably constitutes the first link in the chain of opinions which was to bring Lautréamont's poem to a wider audience. Perhaps it was de Gourmont's piece that introduced *Maldoror* to one of its most brilliant disciples, Alfred Jarry, who was then a young student, on the verge of writing *Ubu Roi* and inventing the Maldororesque "science" of Pataphysics.

The true dawn of Lautréamont's fame, however, did not come until 1920 when Blaise Cendrars, who was then director of the Editions de la Sirène, republished *Maldoror* with a preface by Remy de Gourmont. Since that time new editions, prefaces, critical articles and books, polemics and biographical essays have become increasingly numerous. The stature of Lautréamont has risen steadily until now he stands not very far behind Rimbaud as a prophet of the twentieth century's techniques of cultural revolt.

After having been monopolized by the surrealists, who used and abused *Maldoror* as a bible for their cult of symbolic cruelty and their trust in automatic writing, Lautréamont is now becoming a text for the new cultural radicalism in France. In the film *Weekend* Godard shows one of his revolutionaries walking through the woods near a romantic lake, reciting *Maldoror* aloud, as if the uncompromising violence of the poem were an ancestral voice calling forward to *The Damned of the Earth*, and Frantz Fanon's theories of revolutionary violence.

From a formal point of view it is not quite accurate to call *Maldoror* a poem. In fact it is hard to know how to describe it. Many episodes have the taut composition of Baudelaire's *Petits Poèmes en Prose*, or Aloysius Bertrand's *Gaspard de la Nuit*. They are dense, compacted, almost lyrical tales, in which argument, storytelling and startling imagery combine to create an effect of Gothic horror. On the other hand, many sections are not stories at all, but rather meditations of a sort, or mock-confessions. And interspersed with these are fragments which develop the mood of the popular literature of the time, those interminable feuilleton novels mentioned earlier. In fact *Maldoror* seems to locate itself at the crossroad of all the genres, expressing quintessentially all the possibilities of the late romantic spirit in an unprecedented blend of forms, which constitutes a new form.

The work has no obvious formal unity. It is divided into six larger sections named *Chants*, or Cantos. But each of these in turn is divided into a number of subsections in which various of the above formal characteristics predominate. In a sense *Maldoror* perpetually begins again, starting up from scratch, section after section. Nonetheless one is never distracted by a sense of fragmentation. Although there is no formal unity, and although the subsections of each Canto follow each other in what is apparently a random order, the mood is never broken. The reader moves from beginning to beginning, as if in fact he were getting somewhere. The imperious rhetoric of the poem accounts for this. As we read we feel that we are being dealt with, guided in some indefinable way.

Indeed there are changes which become apparent as one reads. The frankly romantic epic of God versus Maldoror, the sadistic rebel against the frigid deadly father, is more prominent in the earlier Cantos. It is gradually replaced by passages of mock rhetoric in which the reader's attention is conducted through absurd loops of reasoning and nonargument, into which are woven flashes of stunning violence and humor. Imbedded in this taffylike prose one encounters a current of self-destructive fantasies, often describing what seem to be hallucinations. Increasingly urgent reflections appear on the nature of sanity, expressing both a fear of madness and resentment against the requirements of sanity.

Then, with the Sixth Canto, there is a break. Lautréamont casts a glance backward over the preceding Cantos and detects a flaw which apparently frightens him, as if, instead of beginning again, episode by episode, *Maldoror* had acquired a psychic unity which had evolved strangely downward:

> You, whose enviable calm can only embellish your face, don't think I'm about to go on exclaiming at the top of my voice, like some child in the third grade, in stanzas fourteen or fifteen lines long that must seem out

of place; the sonorous slurpings of Indochinese chickens, as grotesque as anything you could dream up, if you really tried. . . . There won't be any more blasphemies, with the specialty of making you laugh; fictive personalities that should have stayed home in the author's brain cells; or nightmares placed far too high above ordinary existence. . . . (321)

All of the final Canto is then devoted to an elaborate parody of one of those popular feuilleton novels, complete with mysterious passwords, plots, counterplots, and key phrases which become absurdly clear later on in the action. The culmination occurs when Maldoror drills a bullet into the head of God, who has changed Himself into a rhinoceros. Then, from the top of the column on the Place Vendôme, he whirls his victim, Mervyn, over the rooftops of Paris to his resting place on the dome of the Panthéon, where he will crown the immortal heroes of France with his ridiculous skeleton.

The ending of *Maldoror* is a nonending, just as its beginnings were nonbeginnings. The shape of the poem is circular, but in a special way. Perhaps Lautréamont himself hit on the most accurate description of his formal triumph in *Maldoror*:

Flocks of starlings have a way of flying that is unique, and seems to follow a uniform, regular tactic, like that of a disciplined troop obeying with precision the voice of one leader. The starlings are obeying the voice of instinct, and their instinct tells them to fly ever closer to the center of the pack, while the speed of their flight carries them always beyond it, so that this multitude of birds, magnetized toward a single point by their common inclination, perpetually coming and going, flowing and crossing over in every direction, forms a manner of extremely agitated whirlwind, whose entire mass, without following any precise direction, seems to have a general movement of rotation on itself, resulting from the particular circulatory movements of each participant, in which the center, tending always to be displaced, but continually pressured and pushed backward by the contrary force of the surrounding lines which weigh upon it, is always denser than any of those lines, which, in turn, are increasingly dense the closer they are to the center. Despite this unusual whirlwind movement, the starlings traverse the ambient atmosphere with extraordinary speed, winning second by second their precious way toward the end of their fatigue, and the goal of their pilgrimage. You too, reader, don't pay any attention to the strange way I have of singing my stories. (285-6)

It is a fitting touch of buffoonery that Lautréamont's mock-elaborate description of the starlings in flight (and his poetry in progress) is lifted word for word from Dr. Chenu's naturalist encyclopedia, a popular work of the time. That too, perhaps, is part of Lautréamont's *tourbillon*, the comic-grotesque whirlwind out of which Isidore Ducasse managed to speak to us.

III

Perhaps the most intriguing, and least solvable, of the mysteries concerning Isidore Ducasse is that of his identity. Nothing, or almost nothing, is known of his life beyond the barest outlines; and there seems to be little hope of unearthing new information. For some time he was confused with an anarchist agitator, a certain Frederick Ducasse, who made a name for himself during the Commune and was described by Jules Vallès in *L'insurgé*. This confusion, based on no evidence whatsoever beyond their common name, created a convenient label for the energies of *Maldoror*. The surrealists, themselves committed to channeling their cultural revolution into politics, were surely disappointed when that discovery, like so many other "facts" about Isidore Ducasse, was volatilized.

A number of lurid traditions circulated at one time or another concerning the Ducasse family. Stories were told of their hereditary insanity, mysterious suicides, sadistic love affairs involving the father, the son, and anyone else who bore the mysterious family name. They have all been radically disproven. In fact the closer one approaches to the rare facts of Isidore Ducasse's passage on earth the less there seems to be to tell.

He was born in 1846, in Montevideo, Uruguay, son of a French embassy clerk, François Ducasse, who had emigrated to South America some years earlier, from the Pyrenée region of southern France. François Ducasse eventually become chancellor of the embassy, and was a respected, wealthy citizen of the French colony in Uruguay. Ironically enough, François Ducasse, in later years, devoted himself to publicizing the positivist philosophy of Auguste Comte. He lectured on the subject and even founded the first Temple of Reason in South America.

Perhaps there is a biographical hint contained in this fact. A link of psychic conflict surely exists between the rational father and the compulsively unrational son, a conflict which appears all the more profound when we call to mind Isidore Ducasse's literary "method," which used the high, balanced rhetoric of the "father" while turning it aside into such subversive byways of subject matter. But the hint is really no more than that. No evidence has been found to indicate a durable split between the father and the son. Until his death Isidore Ducasse lived comfortably on the allowance his father gave him, and that allowance was apparently not discontinued even after the First Canto of *Maldoror* had appeared in 1868. We can only suppose that François Ducasse, though he may have been shocked by his son's peculiar imagination, was at least intrigued with the idea that his son was becoming a writer. The only reference to his father comes in a letter Isidore Ducasse wrote to his banker, and it is hard to know what to make of it:

> You have decided to apply the unfortunate system of distrust suggested vaguely by my father's bizarre notions; but you can see that my headaches do not prevent me from considering carefully the difficult position into which you have been put by a sheet of letter paper from South America, the main fault of which is its lack of clarity; because I don't count the inappropriateness of certain melancholy remarks, easily excused in an old man, and which, on first reading, seem to impose on you the necessity, in the future, of modifying your strict role as a banker vis-à-vis a person who has come to live in the capital. (397-8)

Aside from telling us that Ducasse was subject to bad headaches, the letter certainly expresses resentment; and the tone of it is not reassuring. It is full of meandering, half-controlled sentences which do not seem quite pitched for a banker's ear. But then it is not hard to understand the defiance a boy like Isidore Ducasse might feel for the starched formality of bankers and fathers. Most of us have talked that way at one time or another. In any event it appears that the funds were never cut off.

On the other hand, according to the accounts of people who knew François Ducasse during the decade or so after Lautréamont's death, he never mentioned his son's literary activity, saying only that the boy died in France. One makes of that what one wishes. Was the father ashamed, and shocked by the strangeness of *Maldoror*, or embarrassed at the fact that his son's literary career had been so unsuccessful (everything Lautréamont published in his lifetime, *Maldoror* and the two small volumes of *Poésies*, was paid for by the author). Or was he simply indifferent? There is really no way to know.

As for Isidore Ducasse's mother, we know that she died eighteen months after his birth, and so never entered into his life in any positive way. Attempts have been made to prove that she committed suicide (again the fascination with Lautréamont's supposed madness), but the recently discovered fact that her funeral was held under the auspices of the Church seems to eliminate that possibility.

There have been several biographies of Lautréamont but they are largely works of imagination, forcing a great deal of connective fantasy into place between the few known facts. Much has been made, for example, of the fact that Ducasse was born and raised during an extremely troubled period in the history of Uruguay. Montevideo, during much of the 1840s and '50s, was under siege by Argentinian troops. There had already been a history of bloodthirsty conflict between the countries, and books describing the troubled period are filled with stories of gratuitous bloodbaths worthy of Lautréamont himself. Thus, it is claimed, Lautréamont imbibed the language of heartless violence during his earliest years, storing it up until his literary vocation declared itself years later. There are indeed a number of references to sieges, famine, plague and revolution in *Maldoror*, and these could well be connected to memories of his childhood. But the references are never particularized. They form part of the somber

rhetoric of the book, without seeming to be in the least autobio-
graphical. Anyway that kind of connection between life and
literature is surely banal; it can tell us little about the literary
coherence of the poem. Neither does it offer any reliable answers
to the more specifically biographical question, why, of all memories, would Isidore Ducasse have chosen just those to form the
material of his poetry? The mystery remains intact.

When he was fourteen, in 1859, Isidore Ducasse was sent back
to France by his father to continue his education. He spent the
next six years at the imperial lycées of Tarbes and Pau, where
records show that he was a reasonably hard-working, successful
student, somewhere near the top of his class in most disciplines,
but by no means outstanding. There is evidence that Ducasse
may have returned to Montevideo for a few months in 1867 or
1868. He was issued a passport in Bordeaux and seems to have
sailed for South America on a boat named *The Harrick*. In the
First Canto, written around that time, he says, "Not long ago I
saw the ocean once again, and walked upon the deck of ships; the
memories are as alive as if it had been yesterday." (136) Whether
or not this constitutes evidence remains to be seen. As a matter
of fact it seems at the least risky to use *Maldoror* biographically
at all. The tone of the work is so rhetorical, the episodes are so
completely subject to the transformations of fantasy, the "con-
fessions" it makes are so obviously impersonal, that whatever
hints one gleans from the book must be thoroughly substantiated
from outside sources. This means that such questions are all but
closed, since there are no outside sources, beyond the minimal
records of birth certificate, death certificate, the archives of a
lycée, and a few meager letters. To be sure there exist some
observations recorded many years later from people who apparently knew Isidore Ducasse, but their reliability seems question-
able in every case. Nonetheless they are all we have, and will be
transcribed, for what they're worth, a bit further along.

The final period in the life of Isidore Ducasse began when he
moved to Paris (probably toward the end of 1867) where he
seems to have remained until his death. None of the commonly
"known" details of Ducasse's existence in Paris have been substantiated by facts of any kind. It became axiomatic, for ex-

ample, in the 1920s, that he was poor, lived an isolated, bohemian existence, knew no one, drank lots of coffee, and composed
Maldoror with the help of a piano. This picture of a nervous,
defiant and yet victimized hero of the poetic wars simply does
not hold up. As we have seen, he was amply supported by his
father, even to the point of being able to pay substantial sums
out of his own pocket for the publications of his work. He lived
during all his time in Paris in the neighborhood of the Grands
Boulevards, on Rue du Faubourg, Montmartre, and Rue Vi-
vienne. This was a fashionable, lively neighborhood at the time,
not the sort of place a poverty-stricken poet could well afford.

Ducasse may or may not have been isolated during those years.
In a letter to his banker, he writes, "You can find me in at any
time of the day." This could mean either that he never went out
and lived his last years miserably alone, or that he wrote steadily
during the day and went out only in the evening. We do know
that Ducasse had some literary contacts. Shortly after the First
Canto of *Maldoror* was published in August 1868, a mention of
the poem appeared in a small magazine, *La Jeunesse*, which was
run by a young writer about Ducasse's age, named Alfred Sircos.
The review (the only one to appear of Lautréamont's work in his
lifetime) is quite favorable, and its appearance so shortly after
Maldoror was published implies that Ducasse and Sircos knew
each other.

Again it seems that the picture one gets of Ducasse's life,
though admittedly vague to an extreme, lacks any unusual features. Outwardly Ducasse appears to have led precisely the sort
of existence one might expect of a young, unknown poet, recently arrived in Paris, with a fair supply of money and no
previously established friendships.

As for the piano, the only evidence for it is from Louis
Genonceaux, who never knew Lautréamont, and got his information second hand from Lautréamont's first publisher, Albert
Lacroix. Lacroix had been a well-known publisher in the 1860s
who spent and lost fortunes of money in a deal with Victor
Hugo. How reliable can he be about a poet he published at
author's cost twenty years earlier, perhaps without even reading
the poem he contracted for?

In the end it seems that the only piece of inward biography we have concerning Isidore Ducasse is contained in the letter quoted a page or so back. He was subject to chronic headaches and believed, at least sometimes, that his father was a meddlesome old man—certainly very little to base any biographical speculation on.

The last "event" of Lautréamont's career in Paris, before his death in November 1870, is no less enigmatic than everything else we know about him. In February 1870, he wrote in a letter to the publisher Verboeckhoven:

> You know, I've given up my past. I sing only about hope now; but to do that, I first have to attack the doubts of the century (melancholy, sadness, sufferings, despairs, lugubrious barkings, artificial evils, childish pride, cute maledictions, etc.). In a book I plan to bring to Lacroix at the beginning of March, I criticize the best poetry of Lamartine, Victor Hugo, Alfred de Musset, Byron and Baudelaire, and I correct them in the sense of hope; I show how they should have done it. (400)

A few weeks later he "explains" this change in his literary point of view in a letter to his banker, Darasse:

> I published a book of poems with M. Lacroix. . . . But when it was already printed, he refused to release it because it described life in colors that were too bitter, and he thought he might be prosecuted. It was something like Byron's *Manfred* and the *Konrad* of Mickiewicz, but much worse. . . . Well, that opened my eyes. I said to myself: since the poetry of doubt . . . has reached such a point of empty despair and theoretical evil, then it must be radically false, because it argues about first principles, and they must never be argued about! . . . The poetic groanings of this century are nothing but hideous sophisms. To sing about pain, sadness, melancholy, death, shadow, darkness, etc., is to insist at all costs on seeing the puerile underside of things. Lamartine, Hugo, de Musset voluntarily turned themselves into small-time females. They're the Great-Soft-Heads of our time. Always sniffling. That's why I've completely changed my method, singing only about *hope, calm, happiness, DUTY.* . . . (401)

The sudden change is mystifying, and one hardly knows what to make of it. After having explored the savagery of the "human heart," Isidore Ducasse reverses his field, and stands up extravagantly for Reason, Virtue, and Hope. This would be the theme of

Poésies which Ducasse published in two installments, during the months preceding his death. I doubt that such a rage for orthodoxy has ever been expressed in any literature. Lautréamont castigates doubt, dreams, scepticism, suffering and all literature that speaks of it, atheism, questionings of any kind, insomnia.

Poésies I begins with a declaration of principle: "I replace melancholy by courage, doubt by certainty, despair by hope, evil by good, complaints by duty, sophisms by cold calm, and pride by modesty." (361) From here the argument builds in a series of increasingly wild paragraphs, each one asserting the absolute primacy of first principles, the superiority of moralistic commentary over whatever it comments on, the inherent abjectness of any literature that describes the passions. In a sense, the mode of *Poésies I* is not argument at all, but catechism:

> The poetic groanings of this century are nothing but sophisms.
> First principles must be above discussion. There are not two kinds of poetry. There is only one. (361)

But the elements of the ·catechism quickly take on an air of exaggeration. They become sensuous and half-controlled, until one has the sense of reading some strange mirror reflection of *Maldoror* itself. Ducasse writes, in *Poésies*: "Not everyone is capable of extremes, in one sense or the other." (366) But if there is one thing Isidore Ducasse is capable of, it is extremes. Indeed one wonders if he was capable of anything else. In *Poésies* he appears to have crossed over the moral universe to its other side, where he continues to trace his signature of verbal wildness. His moral catechism is no less extraordinary than his antimoral epic:

> It's easy to describe the passions: all you need is to be born a little jackal, a little vulture, a little panther. (363)

> Yes, good people, I want you to hear me: take a red-hot shovel and a little yellow sugar, and burn the duck of doubt with lips of vermouth, spreading tears which do not come from the heart in a melancholy struggle between good and evil; without a pump, it makes a vacuum everywhere. (369)

> A good criticism of Voltaire's works (meditate the word criticism) is better than the works themselves—naturally. (364)

When he begins to list the forbidden subject matter, the energy
of his words seems to be tempted back across the gulf he has
created. It generates a tremor of sympathy for the proscribed
emotions. If we are to believe that extremes touch each other in
unexpected ways, then Lautréamont is evidence for that fact:

> Disturbances, anxieties, whatever depraves, death, exceptions in the
> moral or physical order, the spirit of negation, stupefactions, hallucina-
> tions served by will power, torments, destructions, overturnings, tears,
> instabilities . . . reek of wet chicken, whatever is faded, frogs, squid,
> sharks, desert wind, whatever is somnambulistic, shady, nocturnal,
> somniferous, night-walker, viscous, talking seal, equivocal, tubercular,
> spasmodic, aphrodisiac, anemic, one-eyed, hermaphrodite, bastard, al-
> bino, pederast, aquarium and bearded women phenomena . . . perfumed
> chancres, camelia thighs, the guilt of a writer rolling on the slopes of
> emptiness, despising himself with joyous cries . . . before these awful
> hellpits which I blush even to name, it is time for us to react against
> whatever sovereignly shocks and enslaves us. (362)

By the time we reach the end of Lautréamont's Homeric list
(stranger than any catalogue in Walt Whitman or Allen Ginsberg),
we are not sure we understand the "blush." Is it shame, or
suppressed pleasure, or simply the flush of energy? If the quality
of the blush is to be truly Maldororesque, it perhaps must be
understood as all three.

Poésies II pursues the same theme while adding to it a new
mode. The catechism is now carried on in an interminable,
somewhat confused series of proverblike statements. What is
more, these statements often have a familiar ring to them. And
after a while the reason for the familiarity becomes clear. Lautréamont has mixed into his text a slightly rearranged anthology
of dictums and aphorisms borrowed from such great moralists of
the past as Pascal, La Rochefoucauld, Vauvenargues, etc. He has
simply "corrected" the dictums and aphorisms in the sense of
Reason, Hope and First Principles.

Some of the corrections are more like verbal games, inverting a
word or meaning. But others are more fully developed in a spirit
of strange humor. Taking Pascal's famous *pensée* about man who
is so weak-minded that even a fly buzzing can disturb his train of
thought, Lautréamont reversed it:

> The spirit of the greatest man is not so dependent that it can be troubled by the smallest noise of the *Tintamarre* erupting near him. The silence of a cannon isn't needed to interrupt his thoughts, nor the creak of a weathervane or a pulley. The fly can't think too well right now. A man is buzzing in its ears. (391)

Ducasse is not above using even puns (*Tintamarre* was the name of a satirical journal) in the service of his upside-down sermonizing.

But he does not limit himself to sentences from the great moralists. Interspersed in *Poésies* are passages from *Maldoror*, which have undergone the same sort of corrective procedure. For example, in *Maldoror* we read:

> I have seen men . . . weary moralists with the effort to expose their hearts, and bring down upon them the implacable anger from on high.

In *Poésies* this becomes:

> I have seen men weary moralists with the effort to expose their hearts, and spread over them the benedictions from on high.

Here is another example:

> blue firmament whose beauty I detest; hypocrite sea, image of my heart.

which becomes:

> Firmament whose beauty I accept, earth, image of my heart.[9]

The whole of *Poésies* is governed by this peculiar game of moralizing, which is so blatant and exaggerated it is hard to take seriously. In fact a number of critics have interpreted Ducasse's method as an elaborate hoax, an extended irony which gives the *coup de grâce* of ridicule to all moralizing rhetoric. Others have detected a controlled hermetic intention in the text and have attempted to work out a serious exegesis of its peculiarly jumbled form.[10]   Still others have taken its repetitions, its plagiarism, and its incoherence as signs that Isidore Ducasse had entered into the final stages of psychosis.

---

[9] For the above comparisons, see Caradec, *Isidore Ducasse*, pp. 224-5.

[10] Georges Goldfayn and Gérard Legrand, *Poésies*, first annotated edition, *Le terrain vague*, Paris, 1960.

It is most difficult to choose between these opinions. Passages in *Poésies I* especially have the same mad brilliance as the best of *Maldoror*. On the other hand, Ducasse's moralizing is so compulsive and schematic that it seems, ultimately, far more unbalanced than anything in *Maldoror*. Ducasse apparently meant *Poésies* to be an ongoing publication, a sort of one-man periodical which would perform an act of literary hygiene on the corrupted imaginings of the century. But the hygiene was so corrosive it could only cleanse itself out of existence. It is impossible to imagine what *Poésies III* would have been like. In fact the whole enterprise of the work remains a mystery which is not fully explainable either in terms of psychiatry or of controlled literary intention.

It was Isidore Ducasse's last mystery. Shortly after the publication of *Poésies II* he died of unknown causes, in a besieged city, where the cemeteries could no longer accommodate the tide of deaths by starvation, disease and despair. There is no record of his burial, no tombstone, no collection of relics. It seems that he was laid to rest in a portion of the municipal cemeteries which was sold off several years later to private contractors. Somewhere in Paris, a house contains the bones of Isidore Ducasse mingled in its foundations.

What did the man look like? What did his friends think of him? Was he loyal, eccentric, shy, ambitious? Was he generous, or miserly? Did any hint of his inner turbulence show in his mannerisms, on his face? Did he have a lover? Was he an orderly person? Well-dressed, even dandyish? (he could have afforded it.)

There are no reliable answers to these questions. All we know is that he wrote the books we say he did, that he lived, and then died far too young. True, there were some witnesses, and they left their testimony; but how seriously can they be taken?

Albert Lacroix, for example, was Ducasse's publisher for *Maldoror*. In 1890 Louis Genonceaux asked him about Lautréamont, and got the following information (in Genonceaux's words):

> He was a tall, darkish young man, without a beard; he was nervous, worked hard, and lived a clean life. He wrote only at night, seated at his piano, declaiming . . . to an accompaniment of musical chords. This

method   of   composition   was   the   despair   of   the   other
tenants. . . . (11-12)

There is a serious question about Lacroix's reliability, however.
When Genonceaux spoke with him he was an old man, and he
was being asked about an obscure poet he may have talked to
twenty years before, at a time when he was busy with important
publishing ventures involving Zola and Victor Hugo. For all we
know, the person he describes is not Isidore Ducasse at all.
Besides, in a letter to his banker Ducasse mentions that he lived
on the same street as Lacroix's publishing house but that he had
not been there in months—proof that there were no close ties
between the two men.

The other testimony, though more elaborate, is also more
doubtful. In 1920 it was discovered that one of Lautréamont's
acquaintances from the lycée at Pau was still alive. His name was
Paul Lespès, and when contacted he wrote out a long account of
his memories:

> I can still see that tall, thin young man, his back hunched over a little,
> his skin pale, his long hair falling over his forehead, his voice small and
> high. His face wasn't at all attractive.
>   Usually he was sad and quiet, as if he were folded into himself. A
> few times he spoke with me excitedly about the countries beyond the
> ocean, where life was happy and free.
>   He liked Racine and Corneille very much, and above all Sophocles'
> *Oedipus. . . .*[11]

Lespès' testimony goes on at great length, telling how Ducasse
"usually had difficulty expressing himself," that sometimes he
had a way of talking rapidly, nervously. He describes Ducasse's
"strong interest in mathematics," and his migraine headaches
(which we know of also from one of Lautréamont's letters).
Once when they were out swimming together, Ducasse apparently said to him, "I need to come here more often, to cool off
my sick brain in this spring water."

The partisans of Lautréamont's madness were delighted with
another of Lespès' reminiscences:

> The distant attitude he had . . . a sort of disdainful gravity, and a
> tendency to consider himself a being apart, the obscure questions he

[11] Caradec, *Isidore Ducasse,* quoted on p. 76.

shot at us without warning and that we could never answer, his ideas, the forms of his style which our excellent professor Hinstin duly criticized, finally the way he had of being irritated sometimes without any serious reason, all these bizarre traits made us feel that his mind was out of balance. [12]

Lespès tells a number of other anecdotes, including one about a showdown between Ducasse and this Hinstin, who was a classical scholar and a teacher of rhetoric. Hinstin apparently flew off the handle at a composition full of sadistic episodes which Ducasse wrote for him. Ducasse took it badly, because he apparently meant his composition as serious literature and not as an act of disrespect, which was the way Hinstin took it.

It is hard to know what to make of all this. At least some of it seems to have been true (the headaches for example), maybe the physical description. But the whole portrait which Lespès gives is simply too good, it answers too well the sort of image one might expect of a bohemian character. When Lespès wrote it down he was over eighty. The memories are more than sixty years old. He is clearly intrigued at having gone to school with someone who became such a scandalous celebrity, albeit decades after his death. There is a more serious objection, however. In places, Lespès's memories seem to be influenced by his reading of *Maldoror*. The reference to Ducasse's love of mathematics is an example. School records show that Ducasse was quite an ordinary math student. But Lespès had surely read the Ode to Severe Mathematics in *Maldoror*, and may have reconstructed his memories from that.

Another example of Lespès' possible untrustworthiness comes when he tells of Ducasse's great love of nature, especially animal life:

> The animal world greatly excited his curiosity. I saw him once stand for a long time in the park of the lycée, admiring a beetle with strong red coloring. . . . He sometimes questioned us about the habits of different birds in the Pyrenée region, and the way they flew.
>
> He had an observing eye. So I wasn't surprised to read (in *Maldoror* . . .) the remarkable descriptions of cranes, and above all starlings, flying. He'd observed them especially well. [13]

[12] Caradec, *Isidore Ducasse*

[13] Caradec, *Isidore Ducasse*

There is only one trouble with this. We know now that Lautréamont plagiarized those admirable naturalistic descriptions from Dr. Chenu's *Encyclopédie d'Histoire Naturelle*.

The unanswered questions are tantalizing. The attempts at resolving them systematically seem destined to fall short, as if fate had woven a conspiracy around the life of Isidore Ducasse, occasional Count of Lautréamont. And the obscurity of the man's life is ironically matched by the impersonality of his writing. Among all the things *Maldoror* can tell us, the one thing it cannot tell us is who wrote it, what sort of man could have experienced the adventure of those images, and could have mastered it sufficiently to create this great poem.

PART TWO:
The Violent Narcissus

I

For Isidore Ducasse, poetry was an act of deception, a strategy enabling his all-too-human weakness to compound itself into a strength.

Thus when Maldoror approaches a young boy in the Tuileries Gardens, the poet listens to his insinuating voice, and he understands:

> You're still too young to be the strongest one; yet even now you can master the art of deceit, the most beautiful instrument of great men. When the shepherd David struck Goliath in the face with a stone from his slingshot, isn't it remarkable to observe that David overcame his enemy by ruse alone, though if they'd fought hand to hand, the giant would have crushed him like a fly. Well, it's the same with you. (175)

Lautréamont often describes his poem as an act of open hostility, a declaration of war. But Maldoror, whose "wisdom" governs the poem's catastrophic vision, understands the danger of solitary combat. "In open warfare you'll never vanquish man, on whom you long to impose your will; but with deceit, you can fight on alone against all." (175)

We know that Lautréamont imagined himself to be the warrior, fighting "alone against humanity" (252), and his weapon was the most essential of all ruses, language (and poetry), the most beautiful instrument of great men:

> I will not use weapons made of wood or steel; I will spurn with my feet the veins of mineral drawn from the earth: at a touch from my hand, the harp's strong, angelic sound will become a dreadful talisman. (252)

The poet's weapon in *Maldoror* is not the "sucker" or the "tooth" or any fantastic blend of animal aggressions. For Lautréamont, man alone has the doubtful privilege of "totalizing evil,"[1] because man wields the supreme violence through the use of his imagination.

Already at the beginning of the Second Canto, Lautréamont tells how his need to write is closely linked to the struggle he is engaged in with the "All-Powerful." Taking his pen in his hand, he cries out: "But . . . what's wrong with my fingers? The joints get stiff as soon as I begin to write. And yet, I've got to write." (163) A storm breaks out paralyzing the poet; the physical world rises against him.

> Why this storm, and why are my fingers paralyzed? Is this a warning from up there to keep me from writing, and to make me think about the risk I run, distilling the drool from out of my squared mouth? (163)

But the ruse of language enables him to resist God's anger. Soon "the storms attack someone stronger than they are." And when, occasionally, he meets up with the All-Powerful, He "keeps out of my way, to avoid the triple platinum dart that nature has given (me) for a tongue." (166)

Unlike his romantic predecessors, (Melmoth and Satan), Maldoror is essentially a literary hero. Lautréamont never tires of reminding us that Maldoror, whatever else he may be, is "a child of (the) imagination" (162). He *is* because he is literary. For all his cruel magic and his violence, Maldoror himself is not the actual hero. That honor is reserved for his creator, the poet, wielding "his terrible ironies with a hand that is firm and cold." (166)

Before testing the "limits of literature," as Roger Caillois has proposed, Lautréamont is more deeply concerned with testing its function. So often the bizarre fairy tales which compose *Mal-*

---

[1] Bachelard, *Lautréamont*, Corti, Paris, p. 24.

doror turn self-consciously upon themselves, as Lautréamont evokes "these poetic discussions" (216), "this laborious slice of literature I'm composing" (254), "these literary beauties I'm leafing through." (275) Eventually, as the poem develops, Lautréamont's irony will undermine the very words that have created it. But meanwhile he declares his poetry to be "implacably useful." In what way "useful"? How did Lautréamont conceive the function of his poetic armament?

The difficulty is simple. Lautréamont wrote no critical essays, no *art poétique*. The few letters that have survived (to his banker and publisher) are of no help. We have to guide us only *Maldoror*. But that alone is a remarkable document, for Lautréamont, as has been suggested, anchors the most extravagant episodes of his poem in a framework of meditations on the act of literature. His critical lucidity envelops the narrative violence, forming what amounts to a running commentary within the body of the poem. If we are to define Lautréamont's conception of poetry and its implacable usefulness, we will have to be attentive to what happens in the interstices of the poem itself.

But irony and humor are Lautréamont's signature in *Maldoror*. Almost every sentence doubles back on itself, asking a question when it seems to be declaring itself. Even his literary "commentary" dissolves into humor and farce at a moment's notice, warning us that what is serious is also not serious. Nonetheless, Lautréamont justifies our critical desire if we are wary enough and wise enough, because "What our farcical state of mind often takes for a bad joke is merely, in the author's mind, an important truth most of the time." (254)

It seems that humor and truth are inextricable in *Maldoror*.

What exactly is the "usefulness" of poetry for Lautréamont? In a passage describing the "sympathetic employment of metaphor" he tells how this figure of speech "serves the human longing for infinity far more than is usually known by men filled with prejudice and false ideas . . . ." (278) This romantic longing for the "infinite" is an important theme in *Maldoror*. The ocean for Lautréamont has a "moral grandeur" which is an image of "infinity" while man, the ocean's miserable opposite, becomes a figure of impotence whose desires are infinitely frustrated. Another passage describes the same longing in different terms. In his room one night, a child hears the howling of wild dogs tearing each other to shreds in a nearby field. His mother tells him, "When you're in bed, and you hear dogs barking in the fields, do not make fun of what they do: they have an endless hunger for infinity, like you, and me, and all mankind." The poet comments on this strange scene: "Like those dogs, I have a need for the infinite. . . . a need I cannot, I simply cannot satisfy! I am the son of man and woman, or so I have been told. That surprises me. . . . I thought I was far more than that." (134)

Because he cannot bear the frailty of being a man, Isidore Ducasse longs with all his might to be "far more than that." His poem is haunted by images of "radical impotence." (299) Maldoror's muscular wildness bathes, paradoxically, in an atmosphere of frustration and failure. One need only recall the many scenes of symbolic castration (rotting members, hair cut short, heads scalped); or remember Lautréamont's hysterical distrust of sleep and immobility which, nonetheless, gain relentlessly in the poem until they have mastered the world of Maldoror's exploits.

Lautréamont's praise of metaphor, his sense of poetry's "implacable usefulness" refers to, and creates, this contradictory world. The dogs tear each other to shreds because the object of their desire escapes them. But the poet has another strategy. Using the strength of metaphor to challenge his infinite hunger, he assaults the world with "poetry in his fist."

Antonin Artaud once remarked, "Isidore Ducasse always felt a need to drop Isidore Ducasse in favor of the unthinkable Count of Lautréamont, a very beautiful name, a very great name."[2]

Maldoror's status as a "literary" hero corresponds not only to Lautréamont's self-irony and the involuted pleasure he took in undermining the basis of his poem. In addition to his strength and his satanic emotions, Maldoror, the complete warrior, had to be deceptive. He had to brandish the ruse of poetry, and *be* that ruse, so that his "least blow (would) strike home."

We understand now the importance of a passage in the Fourth

[2] Artaud, "Lautréamont n'a pas Cent Ans", *Cahiers du Sud*, n. 275, 30 août, 1946, p. 8.

Canto, where Lautréamont tells the story of a strange creature, half fish and half man, who swims close to a cliff on which Maldoror is standing, looking out over the sea. Maldoror is startled by the appearance of this web-footed creature who stops for a moment, and tells his story:

> For fifteen years I lived in a prison cell, eating nothing but worms and muddy water. I won't tell you about my incredible sufferings during that unjust imprisonment. Sometimes one of my three tormentors would come in suddenly with iron probes and wrenches and other torture instruments. My screams never moved them in the least; my loss of blood made them smile. . . . You can imagine the growing hatred I felt for all mankind . . . .

Then, one day, "through the use of a ruse," he manages to escape:

> Disgusted with the inhabitants of dry land . . . I went down to the beach. . . . Can you believe your eyes? Since the day I left home, I'm not as unhappy as you might think to inhabit the ocean with its crystal caves. I live at peace with the fish, and they bring me what food I need, as if I were their king. . . . (281)

Having learned the art of deception (*la ruse*), the web-footed man escaped from his prison in society and became a spirit of the ocean. Lautréamont's meditation on the uses of metaphor occurs precisely in the midst of this story, as if to formulate, indirectly, a kind of moral. Only by ruse (by poetry) can a man escape from imprisonment in the human, and satisfy his "longing for infinity."

The recurrent image of *le tourbillon* ("the whirlwind") sheds further light on the value of the poetic act for Lautréamont.

In the second episode of Canto II a madwoman appears, whose "face no longer resembles a human face . . . words escape her as she is carried away. . . . by the whirlwind of her unconscious faculties." (227) The woman is no longer entirely human. In her madness, words escape her that seem meaningless. Nonetheless they will be understood, if only by "very few."

The madwoman and the poet resemble each other in many ways. He too will be carried away by a whirlwind; he too must lose his human form (cf: Lautréamont's metamorphoses); he too utters words that "very few" will understand, words that are never far from madness. The connection between the madwoman and the poet is completed when, in the midst of her crazy dance, she drops a roll of parchment, containing the story of a horribly cruel act (that is, containing, in miniature, *Maldoror* itself).

The whirlwind, like the ruse, can also be an instrument of aggression, as in the tale of Falmer. "I grabbed him by the hair with an iron fist, and whirled him around in the air so fast that his hair came off in my hand." (282) There are other examples too. "I could pick you up by the legs, roll you around me like a slingshot, and toss you against a wall." (173) The poem itself ends with the grandiose image of Mervyn whirling endlessly in a circle around the tower of the Place Vendôme (357-8).

The violence of the whirlwind reappears in *Maldoror*, like an obsession.

But enveloping these usages and anchoring them in the imagery of the poem, are passages where *le tourbillon* qualifies the act of poetry itself. At the beginning of Canto V, Lautréamont describes a flock of starlings in flight forming "a kind of happy whirlwind." (285) Lautréamont points out the surprising unity of the birds and their speed, adding: "You too reader, don't pay any attention to the strange way I have of singing my stories." The association is more clearly articulated in the following passage, where Lautréamont describes

> his hungering love that would devour itself if it couldn't seek its nourishment in the realm of heavenly fictions: creating, at last, a pyramid of angels, more numerous than insects squirming in a drop of water, it will weave them together into an elipse and whirl them around it. During this time, a traveler will see . . . a human being carried toward the cave of hell by a garland of living camelias." (220)

The man who hungers for infinity can find his nourishment only in a fiction. In the above passages Lautréamont has provided us with an image to explain what this means. The poet's creations swarm around him in a circle, creating a closed and personal space in the larger space of reality. The whirlwind defines a space of which the poet is the sole center. It is the act of Narcissus. Hemmed in, and expressed, by his images, Lautréamont is literally at the center of the world.

The destructive energies of the whirlwind are ambiguous in a way which characterizes the entire poem. Violence, by its very nature, opens a way beyond forms by fracturing them. It destroys limits, reaches toward the "infinite." But when the violence bends into a whirlwind, it becomes circular, shutting out what is beyond it, replacing the world by a circular image of violence itself. The language of Lautréamont's poem serves his "hunger for infinity"; yet it speaks, paradoxically, in a space that has been limited, closed off.

The art of words, the satanic violence, and the play of the unconscious mind all are merged into a single idiosyncratic energy by *le tourbillon* whose movement creates the larger movement of the poem itself.

We have seen that language, for Lautréamont, was a ruse, a behavior (and the only one possible) that would bolster his chances to survive against the powers of the world. The Great Adversary falls into the snare of Lautréamont's irony and must acknowledge his "triple platinum . . . tongue." But the poet, wielding his special armament, goes one step further. He peoples his poetic world. His irony slices beyond the presence of the Adversary to attack a more immediate, more humble victim, the reader, whom Lautréamont continues to invoke as an audience without which his poetic spectacle could not be said to exist.

In the first sentence of the poem, the reader is a pilgrim, encouraged by the author to "become hard and momentarily ferocious like what he reads," if he is to find "his way through the empty swamplands of these pages." (123) Elsewhere he is a witness before whom the poet "proposes, . . . to declaim in a loud voice the cold and serious stanza you are about to hear." (135) He is also the student who is advised not to become "mired down in the membraned carapace of an axiom you think is unshakeable." (287)

Above all the reader is a victim, sacrificed to the poem's involuted rhetoric, trapped and massacred by its logic, charmed by its images. He is the essential prey. All those fantastic victims which inhabit *Maldoror* are masks for this other, half-dissimulated target, the reader himself.

> To put together mechanically the brain of a somniferous tale, it is not
> enough to dissect stupidities, and to drug the reader's intelligence with
> ever renewed doses, so as paralyze all of his faculties for the rest of his
> life. . . . (353)

Maldoror is meant to be a spectacle, staged for the reader, aimed
at seducing and terrifying him. It is a theater of cruelty, and the
reader

> should at least be grateful for the interest I've shown by allowing your
> presence at these theatrical scenes, which seem to me worthy of
> exciting real attention on your part. (314)

Louis Genonceaux tells how Lautréamont sat at his piano late
at night declaiming his sentences to the accompaniment of musi-
cal chords. Genonceaux probable made the story up, and yet it
has a ring of truth. The poet is a deceiver who stages a dream of
power before the world. He dances and he sings his dream until
the audience is bound by the sorcery of this other strength, made
of ruse and deception, that is, made of literature.

If we are right to consider *Maldoror* as a mode of theater, we
should not be surprised by the pure, declamatory style which
characterizes the work from end to end. The fierce formality of
the poem is located well within the French tradition of high
rhetoric reaching from Racine to Baudelaire. For the poet's ruse
to work, his bait must be carefully chosen, and Lautréamont's
symbolic reader knows what he likes. He is a man for whom "the
masterpieces of the French language are speeches for the distribu-
tion of prizes in high schools, and academic speeches." (364)

Lautréamont's need for a poetry whose model is declamatory
creates a limit beyond which his stylistic versatility will not go.
The spectacle of *Maldoror* includes its audience, because it speaks
a language they know. The very quality of Lautréamont's inspira-
tion separated him from the experimental exuberance which had
begun to dissolve the limits of classical prosody in France. The
stylistic freedom of poets like Rimbaud, Corbière, Verlaine and
Laforgue was foreign to Lautréamont. He literally had no *use* for
it.

This very fact reveals a contradiction in *Maldoror*. Lautréamont is condemned to speak the language of those whom he
considers to be his enemies. That is the only way he can set into

motion the "ruse" of literature. And yet, once he has chosen to enter the combat, how can he prevent this very language from judging him as his enemies would have done? The splendor of classical prosody embodies those very powers of morality which Lautréamont's poem intends to destroy.

It is undoubtedly true that words cannot name without also judging. Language is not objective or passive. It sets out grammatical nets; it selects and rejects, heightens or depresses, through the subtle relief of style. Lautréamont's symbolic reader, transformed by *Maldoror* into a student, an audience, a victim, a perverted lover, continues to accuse the poet by whom he has been mastered, and the means of his resurrection is the pure, classical language which has mastered him.

As the poem develops Lautréamont becomes aware of a ghost hovering at his shoulder seeking revenge. In order to survive he must find a way to neutralize this avenging spirit of the reader. When he flees "the human form" into the byway of his famous metamorphoses, he must also flee the human language which pursues him. And yet this very language is the means by which he flees. What Lautréamont calls his "cretinization"—the involuted prose which thickens and all but stops the movement of the final cantos—is, in fact, a massive twisting of style; it is as if, in these portions of his poem, the poet wanted to destroy his tool by crushing the net of grammar and syntax that organizes it.

Maurice Blanchot[3] interprets the encroaching cretinization of *Maldoror* as a tactic of escape, a viscous rhetoric delaying the announcement of a secret which wells up inside the poet, wanting to be said. That is perhaps true. But the "cretinization" works in still another way. By means of it, Lautréamont attacks the root of his fears. In order to keep his secret not only from others but also from himself, he sets out to destroy the powers of language. In order to prevent his "ruse" from collapsing, he demystifies his own words and thereby, paradoxically, undermines the ruse from within. So as not to become the victim of his reader, he "cretinizes" him. That is, he destroys the reader's language and, with it, his own poem. In the end Lautréamont

[3] Lautréamont et Sade, *Editions de Minuit*, Paris, 1949.

chooses to be his own victim so as not to become anyone else's. Despite the elaborate detours of his poetry (*la ruse*), Lautréamont finally meets the fate of those dogs he describes in the Second Canto; crazy for "infinity," they destroy themselves after having wanted to destroy the world.

This instability lies at the heart of Lautréamont's poetic *tourbillon*, taking the form of a corrosive, self-destructive humor. The surrealists were fascinated by Lautréamont's *humour noir* which erupts unpredictably in the poem, revealing an almost ghostly degree of self-consciousness, as if every psychic impulse, every irruption of imagery and madness in the poem were accompanied by an equal and opposite dose of humorous control. Time after time he undermines his own eloquence with a tug of irony, introducing commentaries or comic details which puncture the rhetoric, turning his own "spectacle" into a joke:

> Excuse me, I thought my hair was standing up on my head; but it's nothing, because, with my hand, I can easily smooth it back in place. (126)

> I don't know what I meant to say just now, because I can't remember the beginning of my sentence. (297)

> I'm going to lie down now, because I need the rest; then, powerfully aided by my hand, once again I will take up the pen which my fingers had let fall. (326)

Behind the "unthinkable" Count of Lautréamont we discover Isidore Ducasse; behind the poet's frantic parade of "fictions" we discover the man himself, unable or unwilling to believe even his own stories.

Having studied the "implacable usefulness" of poetry for Lautréamont, we now discover the limits of that poetry. Nor should we favor one of these aspects over the other as the surrealists were tempted to do. The poem, surely, must "act" before it encounters its limit. And if it collides with that limit over and over again, surely the very collapse of its language must generate a power to haunt and to speak. *Maldoror* will inevitably be torn between Lautréamont and Isidore Ducasse, between the ruse and the ruse unmasked.

These contradictions become more apparent as the poem develops. The ironic density thickens, the work of "cretinization"
takes up more and more narrative room. Lautréamont finds it
increasingly difficult to stand firmly at the center of his poetic
"whirlwind." And as the rhythm of the poem changes, there is a
corresponding change in the spirit of his "commentary."

We have seen how Lautréamont has insisted on the "literary"
quality of his imagination, carefully avoiding the claims of fic-
tional realism. He never tries to convince us that Maldoror's
exploits "really happened." On the contrary Lautréamont has
made a point of reminding us that his only weapon, (his "fearful
talisman") is the poem itself. But now the "danger" his language
has created forces him to employ the ultimate ruse. Bringing the
story of the web-footed man to a close, he declares unexpectedly
that "everything which happened on that summer's night was
real." (281) And again, a bit further on, while Maldoror lies
paralyzed by an agonizing dream, he cries out: "We are no longer
in the story. . . Alas! we have come into reality." (313) By this
final ruse the poet tries to neutralize the "secrets" which spring
into life as he writes. For he is no longer the one who is
dreaming. Those fantastic creatures surrounding him and expressing his most hidden needs are not mirrors in which he sees
his own face (a face that would drive him to despair if he
recognized it). Not at all. The poet has told only what he saw. He
is not the guilty one, nor is he the creator, because all this is
"real." Thereby the poet opens an escape hatch in his own
poem.

But Lautréamont's undermining humor will not allow him
even this ruse. His life is bound to his poem. If on the one hand
he corrodes his language, on the other he is committed to
reinvent it, as the above passage ironically suggests:

> Alas! we have come into reality . . . and although I could put an
> exclamation point at the end of each sentence, that perhaps is not
> sufficient reason not to do so. (314)

He will indicate "reality" by exclamation points. Punctuation
will give the final stamp to what is real. Again the poet's irony
has caught him in the net of language and syntax. Lautréamont

will never reach the silence; although, by the end of the poem, neither Lautréamont or Maldoror will exist. With the harsh words, "Wake up, Maldoror!" the whirlwind of images vanishes. "He woke up as he was ordered to do." (320) But "he" is no longer the same. "He" is now Isidore Ducasse, awakening alone, in his poem. By the end of the Fifth Canto, all the ruses have been tried; now, the poet is indeed in "reality." His language no longer expresses the hypnotic powers of imagination; it has become transparent, truly narrative, describing a moment which has been "lived." This is the moment when the poet "wakes up," unable to fly into fantasy, struggling once more with his all-too-human weakness, as he waits "for the dawn to bring a change of scene, a paltry comfort to his shattered heart." (320)

When he takes up his story again, in the Sixth Canto, and later in *Poésies*, his judgments will be simplified, unilateral. From now on he will be concerned only with certainties. His previous work will seem to him nothing but "the sonorous slurping of Indo-chinese chickens" (321), "fictive personalities that should have stayed locked up in the author's brain cells." (322) Lautréamont's hieratic "theater" will be replaced by a rhetoric that has no use for the ambivalence of the earlier cantos.

In place of a literature that "acts" we will find literature purely and simply, the artifice without the ruse. There will be no "whirlwind of unconscious faculties," no "vomit pouring from inside (my) skull," (219) Because, "Today (I will) construct a little novel about thirty pages long." Having been a creator, he is now simply an artisan, hoping

> that one of these days I will see the consecration of my theories accepted by one or another literary form. . . . I think, after much experiment, that I have found my definitive formula. It's the best, because it's the novel. (323)

Canto VI reflects an obvious break in Lautréamont's work. He recognizes that his previous "mission" was to attack "man, the creator, and myself." (321) And apparently he has not given up this project. But, "from now on the strings of the novel will animate the three above-named characters. . . ." Now everything will happen between the covers of a book. The forms will continue to move for a time, but the poet, once and for all, has stepped outside his poetic "whirlwind." Or so he hopes.

Isidore Ducasse never managed to write those little "novels" unless one considers the final canto of *Maldoror* to be the first of them, and the last as well, for that matter. Ultimately it is hard to imagine him engaged in such an enterprise, especially when we recall the abrupt change in his viewpoint on the uses of literature which occurs with the Sixth Canto.

During the first five cantos the poet had tried to shed his all-too-human identity, as he made himself into the Count of Lautréamont. And after the psychic shipwreck to which he drove his poem he tries to maintain a shadow of the old game. But now "Lautréamont" has become a mere pen name, a thin disguise for the poet, Isidore Ducasse. (In *Poésies* even the pen name is abandoned and will never be used again.) During the poem's slide into danger Lautréamont had been a character, a magnificent companion for Maldoror himself, perhaps the inward, fantastic face of Maldoror. But now, in the "novel," he is no more than a mask and the question arises, can a mask, a pen name, appease the poet's "hunger for infinity?" Does he not need the wild ambivalence of the earlier cantos, by which an act of literature became an act of war? Lautréamont could not keep on with his series of "novels" because the artifice of literature which composed them was too thin, too sane.

But after the "failure" of *Maldoror* there remained for Isidore Ducasse another ruse and another strategy. He could still use the weapons he knew so thoroughly, but now he would use them to *destroy* hunger and to *erase* the infinite from his poetic universe. Lautréamont had made himself into a creature of "infinity," but in his next and last work, entitled *Poésies*, he would become a creature of the *ordinary*, a defender of what Albert Camus aptly described as "banality."

Once more the poet embraces the powers of language, creating a world shaped to his will. And that will itself has not changed, except that now it has been reversed. The "hunger for infinity" has been replaced, in *Poésies*, by an equally extravagant hatred for "infinity."

Once more the sorcery of language is called forth, but this time it is in the service of a poetry whose extreme "banality" and exaggerated "common sense" is modeled on a style that is truly "made by all, and not by one." It is the style of proverbs and popular aphorisms:

> The poetic groanings of this century are nothing but
>   sophisms.
> First principles must be beyond discussion,
> I accept Euripides and Sophocles; but I do not
>   accept Aeschylus.
> Do not show a lack of elementary respect, or
>   bad taste, toward the Creator.
> Great thoughts come from reason alone!
> Brotherhood is not a myth. (361)

It is a rosary of good sentiments and better logic. As the poet had previously done in *Maldoror*, he constructs the elements of a world he longs for. Once more his language has become packed and slippery. If Narcissus could not project an image of himself as vast as the infinite, he could at least reverse himself and create a world to the measure of his failure. If he is condemned to be ordinary and banal, then banality must take over thoroughly, ruthlessly.

> I do not accept evil. Man is perfect. The soul does not fall. Progress
> exists. The good is irreducible. (375)

Language once more becomes an act of warfare, and poetry, a triumphant "ruse."

II

Lautréamont meant his poetry to "act" at the extreme limit of human possibilities, in an atmosphere rarified by violence and self-distrust. Through the use of the imagination, the poet raised himself into the sphere of the unthinkable.

It remains for us now to grasp the complexity of the imaginary life which proliferates in *Maldoror* with an exuberance rarely equaled in the history of modern poetries.

Let us recall the image employed by Lautréamont to describe his poetic act:

> creating at last a pyramid of angels, more numerous than the insects squirming in a drop of water, (he) will weave them together into an ellipse and whirl it around (him). . . . (220)

He could not describe the geography of his poem more accurately. The poet creates a world which surrounds him as a circle surrounds its center. The energy of the "whirlwind" enhances the immovable center that has shaped it into existence. In fact, the center would not exist without the swirl of movement it has created. For the "whirlwind" is the reality of the central point which otherwise would be a fiction, undistinguishable from the general anonymity of all space.

51

Such a poetic world excludes the possibility of dialogue or dramatic involvement. The poet locates his needs at the center of a private space which resembles him and repeats him infinitely. Even the "dear reader," apparently indispensable to the poet's "theatrical scenes," can be no more than a victim or a spectator, never an interlocutor. He is necessary to the work at hand only as he takes his place in orbit around the life-giving center.

The poet's imagery informs us as clearly as any *art poétique* that a unique event will be enacted in *Maldoror*, the drama of Narcissus. The "whirlwind" defines Lautréamont's "hunger for infinity." It is a hunger for the kind of freedom in which—to use Hegel's description of freedom in his *Esthetic Lessons*—"nothing will be foreign to him, but he will find himself in each thing he sees and touches around him."

Lautréamont recreates here a well-known theme of traditional literatures. The geography of fairy tales and mythological narratives is frequently governed by an image of the world's center.[*] At the "navel" of the world, and only there, a bridge spans the gap between heaven, hell and earth. The ontological levels are linked and the human world itself is defined by the linkage as a complex knot tied at the center of creation, binding together all the powers of this world and the next. The center can be a tree (Yggdrasil of Nordic mythology) or a mountain (Olympus) or a cave (the entry way to Hades). But it also can be some more private place. For certain purposes every house, village or temple can be a center.

Lautréamont, however, works out a unique variation on the familiar image. The center of his poetic world is not consecrated as a hub of social and spiritual values. It is not acknowledged by the community. On the contrary, it is private, and that is precisely the point of it. The center for Lautréamont is a shelter from "public" demands; it is a place of combat against the world of society. Lautréamont's sacred center is none other than the poet himself, a rallying point for his idiosyncratic needs.

Thus the imagination of Narcissus recreates a form common to the traditions of mythology; but it has reversed the form, in order to express a vision in which Narcissus is the only god.

[*] Mircea Eliade, *Cosmos and History*, Harper & Row, N.Y. 1959.

It is nonetheless clear that this simple form cannot by itself account for the proliferating episodes of the poem, nor for its impulse to probe so many varieties of cruelty and grotesque humor. It would be more accurate to say that the "whirlwind" represents an ideal form, a limit toward which Lautréamont propels his imaginary world without ever attaining it. By it Lautréamont tries to impose an order on the chaotic inwardness which the act of writing has released in him. The "form" is effective only so far as it catches into its net all the contingencies which "life" (his irrepressible inward energies) imposes brutally and capriciously. If the form cannot meet this demand, if it cannot open itself to receive the chaotic fact of life itself, then its vision will be dislocated by the weight of the disorder it cannot contain. Like the mythology of a people, a poet's vision must be "universal" or perish; it must be able to find a place for the irreducible facts of experience, or be carried away as a dam is carried away by flood waters.

In *Maldoror* Lautréamont pursues his vision. The poem tells the story (the many stories) of his struggle to impose the requirements of Narcissus upon a recalcitrant universe. That is the meaning we must give to the "fearful talisman," the unique "weapon" which the poet forges in his poem.

Once we have understood this, it becomes clear that Lautréamont's definition of poetry as an act of warfare is only partly accurate. The episodes of *Maldoror* are more complex than that. Love is not less important than warfare. Repentance circles back to undermine the violence. Narcissus in pursuit of his image deploys all his energies and all his deceptions to obliterate the "difference" which separates him from that image.

Lautréamont often names the adversaries he has chosen in his poetic warfare. At the beginning of Canto II, it was "man, that wild beast, and the Creator, who should never have given birth to such vermin." (170) Later, a third adversary appears and we read, "man, the Creator and myself." (321) Of these three adversaries, the first two are more spectacular, but the third is by far the most important. The dramatic changes in *Maldoror* (described so well in Maurice Blanchot's important essay) are due primarily to the discovery of this last interior enemy.

But Lautréamont's trio of adversaries is completed by a fourth, the world of nature itself. Narcissus experiences even nature as a foreign presence which must be attacked and "persuaded" by the poet's violence. Lautréamont's massive weaponry assaults God, society, nature and finally himself.

This universal warfare gives rise to the most spectacular portions of *Maldoror*, but it by no means exhausts the variety of the poem's themes. Often mingled with the violence is a strange eroticism, an unexpected sweetness of love. In such passages Narcissus speaks openly of his search for an image that resembles him, as in the many scenes of friendship and friendship betrayed. The search contains overtones of homosexuality, which come together in the famous episode of the "pederasts incomprehensible." Above all, it contains the poet's gentle fascination with incest.

It will be easier for us to understand the forms of violence in *Maldoror* if we first turn our attention to this "quest for a resemblance" which describes so clearly the poem's central meaning.

Several times Maldoror announces the goal of his strange labor. "I need creatures that resemble me. . . ." (304) More often than not he refers to men as his *semblables,*[5] a word which in English is rendered commonly as brother, neighbor, or fellow man, but which, taken literally means "one who resembles me."

The expression *semblable* is of course a familiar idiom. But it presents Lautréamont with a cruel paradox, forcing him to recognize that men "though they are called my *semblables,* don't seem to resemble me at all until now (if they think I resemble them, why do they hurt me so much?)." (280) The poet is obsessed not only by the cruelty of men, but by this painfully disappointing resemblance.

In Canto II Lautréamont gives us the portrait of a classical Narcissus, a hermaphrodite, soft and effeminate, like the naked boy languishing near a pool of water described by Ovid in the *Metamorphoses.* The hermaphrodite's dilemma is contained, for Lautréamont, in a single sentence: "Exhausted by life, and

[5] For example, pp. 172, 193, 206, 208, 253, 257, 280.

ashamed to walk among creatures that do not resemble him, despair has invaded his soul." (177)

The imaginary world of *Maldoror* is charged with the anguish caused by *semblables* who do not resemble. But the poet's yearning is even more absolute than it appears, for beyond resemblance he insists upon the ultimate closeness of "identity."

In the Ode to Old Ocean, Lautréamont evokes the paradox of disappointed resemblance in the following manner: "Why does (man) look at the face of his brother (*semblable*) with such disgust?" To mankind's treachery, he compares the ocean, "symbol of identity," forever equal to itself. (136-7) Further on he condemns man's contradictory nature by comparing it to the pure beauty of mathematics: "You are always the same. No change, no foul air touches the steep rocks and immense valleys of your identity." (193) Thus, on the one hand the poet evokes a human world made of painful differences, and on the other a purer, more spacious world in which everything is *semblable*, where it is impossible to become "inferior to (one's) own identity." (244)

The above passages, of course, refer less to a personal identity of bodies and characters than to the logical concept of identity. But words often lead an underground life in *Maldoror*, making unreasonable connections, far beyond their apparent significance. The passages where Lautréamont praises the abstract principle of "identity" take on a further meaning when we compare them to other passages where the poet acts with surrealistic violence to provoke a union of bodies, a veritable "identity" of the flesh, sealed in blood.

In Canto I, for example, Maldoror plans to attack one of his *semblables*:

> Feed, oh feed confidently on the tears and blood of the adolescent. Blindfold him, while you tear at his quivering body; then after having listened for hours to his heavenly cries . . . you will rush into the next room, pretending that you have come to help him. (128-9)

Apparently Maldoror cannot act with simple violence. Suddenly his movements soften, his violence becomes tenderness, and then he gives himself a different sort of advice:

> You will untie his hands, with their nerves and veins all swollen; you
> will give sight back to his terrified eyes, and begin to lick away the tears
> and blood. (129)

A great deal remains to be said about the symbolic importance of
"tears" and "blood" in *Maldoror*, their role as universal liquifier,
a comforting, if deadly, flood uniting all the forms of life in their
catastrophic element. For the moment let us remark simply that
the violent aggressor has reversed himself and become a tender
aggressor. Maldoror binds up his victim's wounds. Apparently his
awful attack was meant only to provoke this excess of
tenderness:

> Adolescent, pardon me. Once we have left this changing life, I want us
> to be wrapped in each other's arms for eternity; to form one being, our
> mouths glued together forever. (129)

Maldoror dreams of creating an erotic oneness with his victim,
their two bodies sealed together for "eternity." His violence here
defines the inner limit of all resemblances. It extends to the point
of identity.

A theme as humanly rich as the quest for a resemblance must
inevitably evoke a number of subsidiary themes which link it to
the larger movement of the poem. We have seen, for example,
how Lautréamont's characteristic violence is bound up with the
narcissistic quest. Let us consider another episode now, where
the quest for a resemblance appears in a somewhat different
light, in the story of Maldoror's copulation with a female shark.

The episode begins with a phrase already quoted: "I looked
for a soul that resembled me, and couldn't find one." After
having tried, with no success, to appease his "hungering love" in
the world of men, Maldoror sits down "on a rock near the sea."
But while he sits disconsolately on his rock, an extraordinary
adventure begins to unfold before his eyes. He sees a ship
foundering in the midst of a tempest. Slowly the ship and its
occupants are destroyed as Maldoror looks on surprised, and then
delighted. The story of the foundering ship continues to the
intermittent refrain: "The ship in distress shoots off cannon
shots of alarm; but it sinks slowly . . . majestically." Then suddenly Maldoror sees a shape swimming in the distance, "a huge
female shark," come to get her share of the carnage.

He watches this new spectacle "with a growing emotion which he had not felt until then." At last, unable to look on any longer, he leaps into the sea, "holding in his hand the steel knife that never leaves him." The carnage continues in the blood-stained waters around the ship, until finally Maldoror and the female shark are face to face.

> They looked into each other's eyes for a few minutes, each one surprised to find the other's gaze so fierce. . . . Then, with one movement, they slipped closer under the water . . . longing to contemplate his own living portrait for the first time. (210)

Ovid's Narcissus found his image floating on the surface of the water. Maldoror pursues his "living portrait" into "the ocean's depths." He does not look into a mirror, behind which the real waters are concealed; he plunges into the very thickness of the sea. Diving to embrace his "other self," he is accomplishing an act of exuberant life, not one of passive self-destruction, as in the classical legend.

> They fell effortlessly against one another . . . embracing with dignity and gratitude, in a hug as tender as that of a brother and sister. Carnal desires followed quickly upon this show of friendship. Two nervous thighs clung tightly to the monster's viscous skin like two leeches; arms and fins enlaced tenderly around the loved one's body. Soon their breasts and throats were mingled in a sticky mass, smelling of sea-weed . . . (as) they came together in a long, chaste and hideous act of love. . . . (211)

Maldoror, swimming in "the depths of the abyss," can at last satisfy his impossible longing. "At last I'd discovered someone who resembled me."

As happens frequently in *Maldoror*, the adventure of love secretes around it an element of water and blood mingled together, as if this terrible liquidity were somehow necessary to the quest for a resemblance. In the episode where Maldoror assaults an adolescent boy, the scene there too is flooded by a mixture of tears and blood. Apparently it is true, as Lautréamont remarks on one occasion, that "some liquid or other" is necessary if the longing of Narcissus is to be satisfied.

Above all the story of Maldoror's encounter with the female shark reveals a circumstance that will shape the energies of the poem. The "living portrait" which Maldoror discovers in the ocean's depths is not human, and yet he recognizes it as his own. Beyond his *semblables*, beyond the victims served up to his "perverse" instincts, Maldoror discovers the most essential of resemblances. It is one which links him to all the forms of life and violence, proposing an ideal of instinctual liberation which the "human form" alone could not sustain. This discovery, accomplished early in the poem, foreshadows the strangest, most exotic adventure of *Maldoror*, that of Lautréamont's renowned metamorphoses.

The episode of the female shark illustrates still another aspect of Lautréamont's poetic endeavor. It demonstrates the sort of underground alliance which his stories and images maintain with each other, forming a background and a secret architecture beneath the apparent randomness of the poem's thematic organization. The encounter with the female shark enacts an unexpected confession. Much earlier in the poem, Maldoror, for no apparent reason, had cried out, "If it had been up to me, I would have wanted to be the son of a female shark." (134) But that is the very creature which Maldoror has discovered not as a mother but as a lover whose passions give rise to the sought for "identity." Maldoror's act of love, in addition to its obvious extravagance, is also, after its fashion, an incest.

It seems inevitable that Maldoror's narcissistic quest should involve such maternal fantasies which soften and console him in the midst of his compulsive violence. But the presence of the mother is filled with contradictions. Her appearance is almost always bathed in a sentiment of disquiet, as an object of revolt or distrust on the part of her son. She resembles the Terrible Mother of mythologies. But there are times when the symbolic connections loosen and become indirect. Then, almost inaudibly, like an echo, one recognizes the enveloping, tender mother who once had immersed her son in the pleasing life of "identity."

There are many passages in *Maldoror* where the ambivalence of the maternal images appears. The poet speaks of men "whose strongest fist is raised against the sky, like a child's, already perverse, against his mother." (127) Or again, with more precision, "[Men] will advance with great strides, led forward by the spirit of revolt, against the day of their birth, and the clitoris of their impure mother." (248)[6] Even in Maldoror's encounter with the female shark, where the theme of incest is expressed so loosely, the ambivalence appears. Maldoror dives to meet his "living portrait" with a steel knife in his hand.

But several times the incestuous feelings are dramatized more openly, as in a curious passage where Maldoror remembers how his "face [was] madly kissed by all the mothers." (182) Or in this other passage, where he tells how man "would rather have death for a mother than remorse for a son; plunging his head up to the shoulders in the earthy complications of a hole." (214) It is scarcely coaxing the image, to see a phallic symbolism in the head plunged into a hole in the maternal earth as if to be reborn in reverse.

Elsewhere Lautréamont describes some truly curious scenes between mothers and sons. In a story which apparently echoes Goethe, Maldoror attempts to seduce a young boy as he sits at home one night with his mother and father. Little by little the family becomes aware of an ambient menace which seems to weigh heavily upon them. The father struggles to preserve the tranquility of his home by whispering prayers. But then, a voice is heard: "Radiant angel, come to me. . . . My magnificent palaces built with walls of silver, golden columns and gates of diamond. . . ." It is Maldoror speaking in dream to the young boy. But as the story continues the enticements of Maldoror become confusing. It becomes increasingly difficult to know syntactically who is speaking, who is enticing and seducing. Is it Maldoror, or is it the mother's secret thoughts emerging in this way? In fact midway through the story, the mother's voice seems to fade away, as if she were leaving her place to these seductive words which express her more deeply than she could express herself. Still the son refuses to give in until Maldoror shouts at him angrily: "Since you won't listen to me, I'll make you cry and grind your teeth, like a hanged man." (144-50) At which point, mother and son fall down dead.

Is it not possible to read this episode as a dream of incest, veiled and yet half-expressed, by the grammatical ambiguities?

[6] See also pp. 123, 129, 188, 192, 214, 288.

That interpretation is unexpectedly seconded later in the poem
when we come upon the story of a young man hanging by his
hair, who is, in fact, crying and grinding his teeth. Maldoror cares
for his wounds, and learns from his own mouth the cause of this
strange punishment:

> He told me how, one evening, his mother had called him into her room
> and ordered him to undress so that he could spend the night with her in
> bed. (262)

Because he refused, his mother chastised—or, should we say,
castrated—him, causing him to be hanged from a tree by his hair.

The two stories complete each other unexpectedly. In one a
son is damned, in the other the malediction is accomplished.
Once again, as in the story of the female shark, the poet allows us
to spy a web of hidden connections which organize his imagination, constituting a form within the form of the poem.

In both of these stories the incestuous need is frustrated, and
in one of them the failed act is ascribed to a third character who
is clearly not Maldoror. Maldoror presides over the scene but the
sin is not his. Lautréamont, although he is fascinated by incest,
must keep it at arm's length if he can. He must confess, but he
must also disguise the erotic energy which drives him through a
world of grotesque imagery toward some hidden principle of his
life.

The fear of incest is closely tied to another of *Maldoror's*
emotional themes, the "radical impotence" which comes to
haunt the poet on so many different occasions. Lautréamont
pursues his vision through alternations of power and impotence,
action and immobility. The incest accomplished evokes the
theme of power, the quest for a resemblance, the sadistic violence, the ocean, the metamorphoses. But failed incest expresses
the dismay and the confusion of impotence. That is how we must
interpret the final scene of the above-mentioned story. The poet
describes the gallows standing in the distance, still bearing the
victim's detached hair:

> When the wolf sees that dark scalp on the horizon, swinging in the
> wind, he doesn't give in to his inertia, instead he runs away with
> incredible speed. (264)

The emblem of punished incest repels the powers of animal life, the principle of liberation and metamorphosis.

Lautréamont's quest for a resemblance involves acts and values of many different kinds. It embodies the "centrifugal force" by which the poet holds fast at the center of his "whirlwind" of fictions. But at the same time it reveals a spirit of weakness, a discouragement which breaks the circle and ruffles the incestuous mirror of Narcissus.

To complete this analysis of the quest for a resemblance it is necessary to evoke a theme which has often been proposed as the most important one in *Maldoror*, perhaps the origin of its frenetic energies. Women are scarce in Lautréamont's poem, although a quantity of young boys, some anonymous, others graced with romantic names, enter into the poem to meet with a variety of fates. One could make an inventory, and a long one, of scenes in which homosexuality is more or less openly evoked. The scenes would reveal the same mingling of tenderness and violence which we have discovered elsewhere in *Maldoror*. All these episodes where homosexuality is alluded to, are drawn together by the famous passage in Canto V, which begins:

> O pederasts incomprehensible, I will not cry insults at your marvelous degradation; I will not cast scorn upon your infundibular anus. (302)

As if to explain the romantic garland of adolescents which surrounds him in the course of his adventures, Maldoror cries out, "No, I simply don't like women. . . . I need creatures that resemble me. . . . Are you really sure the long-haired ones have the same nature as mine?" Even the "dear reader" enters into Lautréamont's erotic mirror-game:

> Why can't I see the one who reads me through these seraphic pages? If he has not passed his puberty, let him come near. Squeeze me up against you, and don't be afraid to hurt me; little by little, tighten the rope of our muscles. More. (303)

The role of the "spectator" in *Maldoror* is now more clearly defined. The poet widens the net of his images, until his audience has been caught in it. The "whirlwind" expands, fattening itself on the life of men and objects, because the hunger of Narcissus has no limit; by its very nature it is insatiable.

Therein lies the source of the apocalyptic energy which feeds the quest for a resemblance and which here is transformed into a vast erotic dream:

> Oh, if the universe could have been a great celestial anus instead of a hell, look at what I'm doing down here, under my belly: yes, I would have poked my stick right up into its bloody sphincter, breaking open the bone with my eager movements. Suffering then would not have blown great dunes of shifting sand over my sightless eyes; I would have discovered the underground cave where truth sleeps on, my rivers of thick sperm would have found an ocean to run to! (303)

Narcissus needs to "resemble" and to become the entire universe: there can be no other partner for his "infinite" desire.

Yet even as the desire is expressed Lautréamont already descends the slope of "radical impotence." When he describes the universe as a narcissistic partner, he writes in the conditional. The dream, after all, is only a hypothesis, and so he ends it:

> But why do I find myself regretting an imaginary state of affairs that will never happen in reality?

Remembering that his vision is only "literary," he encounters that limitation with his usual irony:

> There's no use insisting, I feel it; the opacity of this paper, remarkable in more ways than one, is a serious obstacle to our complete union. (305)

III

A discussion of Lautréamont's quest for a resemblance requires an examination of the way he uses relationships which
bind together a number of otherwise quite dissimilar images and
episodes. These relationships act as "themes" which contribute
to the narcissistic quest: the apocalyptic violence, the metamorphoses, the imagery of fluids and ocean, etc. By questioning
several of these "themes" more directly, it is possible to see in
action, so to speak, the elasticity and suppleness of the strange
self-vision which the poet pursues.

Surely the most striking quality of *Maldoror* is its enveloping
aggressiveness. Not only is Lautréamont aware of his inclination
toward violent imagery, he claims it as the main aim and subject
matter of his poem. The scope of the violence is expressed clearly
in the episode already mentioned describing the "rage" of dogs
crazed for infinity. The aggressive energy in this tale is pure,
unlimited by any object, because the entire universe is its object.
The dogs race angrily across the plain, barking

> against stars in the north and east, south and west; against the moon;
> against mountains far away, that seem like great rocks lying in shadow;
> against the cold air they breathe into their lungs, making the inside of

their nostrils hot and red; against the silence of the night; against owls, whose slanting flight skims against their muzzles, carrying in their beaks a rat or frog, living food, good for the little ones; against rabbits that disappear in the blink of an eye; against the thief who gallops away on his horse when his crime is done; . . . against trees whose leaves, gently swaying, are so many mysteries which their deep, intelligent eyes cannot understand; against spiders suspended by their long legs; . . . against crows who haven't found anything to eat all day, and limp back to their nests with tired wings; against rocks on the shore; against lights which appear on the masts of invisible ships; against the hollow sound of waves; against huge fish swimming with their dark backs in the air, then plunging into the abyss; and against man who has enslaved them. (132-3)

At last their rage against the world exhausts itself, but the world remains, an inscrutable provocation, until finally the dogs turn their exhausted need against themselves, attacking the very root of their despair:

A few hours later the dogs, running around almost dead from exhaustion, will leap on one another without knowing what they're doing. And then they will tear themselves into a thousand shreds with incredible speed. (133)

The tale of the mad dogs is a sort of parable in which Lautréamont explains the violence which he has chosen as the unique vocation of his poem. We have seen how the aggressiveness of *Maldoror* is purely, and precisely, symbolic: the poet's only weapon is his poem. Throughout *Maldoror* Lautréamont goes out of his way to keep this "literary" fact in view. But the dogs too can only bark. Their violence is spoken, not acted out. And when, like the poet, the dogs discover their essential impotence, the only true violence they commit is against themselves. Frustrated, they aim their rage at the only near target they possess, each other; just as, in *Maldoror*, the only violence which attains a real object beyond "literature" is the violence the poet wields, psychically, against himself.

The forms of Lautréamont's aggressive impulse in the poem will become apparent in a description of the apocalyptic warfare waged by his hero against the four adversaries which inhabit his poetic universe: nature, man, the Creator, and himself.

The first of Maldoror's adversaries, "nature," seems hardly to exist at all in the poem. The stories Lautréamont tells are sparse in descriptive detail, like fairy tales or mythological narratives. The world of nature is a conventional backdrop within which the true location of the story is worked out in terms of action and events. The natural world is of course present in the poem in another way. Lautréamont is outstandingly gifted in suggesting the movement and peculiarities of animal life. But that is a subject in itself, and will require attention shortly in discussing the larger theme of the metamorphoses.

Apart from the animal world, the world of nature in *Maldoror*, is stylized and literary, following quite closely the descriptive modes of the Gothic novel. The landscapes of the poem are lush with conventional vegetation. Lotus blossoms, pansies, and roses are all fairly uninventive symbols of peacefulness and innocence. Dry brushwood, thistles and thorns convey loneliness and desolation. The stories invariably take place at nightfall, or in the dark of night, sometimes at dawn. The fields are interrupted by lonely walls along which the hero gallops on his white horse. Many scenes in *Maldoror* could have been written by Beckford or Maturin. This one, for example:

> By moonlight, near the sea, in isolated nooks of the countryside . . . everything takes on forms which are yellow, ambiguous, fantastic. Tree shadows race backward and forward, sometimes very slowly and sometimes faster, flattening themselves out and swooping along the earth. The wind groans a languorous melody through the trees, and the owl sings its grave complaint. . . . (132)

In *Maldoror* as in the Gothic novel the mood of nature becomes a sign, an emblem for the dark commands of "fate" which, although they speak through natural phenomena, are metaphysical.

The attack against nature, therefore, is for the most part a spiritual violence. It belongs to Maldoror's satanic struggle with the Creator. When the hero declares that "the storms attack someone who is stronger than they are," (164) his defiance is directed not so much against the forces of nature as against God Himself. The storms, it appears, are nothing but "agents of (His) celestial police force."

Nonetheless, when nature and its "laws" are evoked independ-

ently in their own right, they are challenged by Maldoror, because their very independence makes them into adversaries:

> So, there is a power stronger than the will. . . . Malediction! The stone
> would like to escape from the laws of gravity? Impossible. (125)

Lautréamont's "whirlwind" has place for only one force,
flowing from a single will, his own. If Maldoror is to be at the
center of his world it is exactly necessary that the stone escape
from the laws of gravity. Maldoror's pure aggressiveness, which
for Bachelard is essentially primitive and muscular, is more like a
will to overcome, a desire for total power. If the hero's will is to
survive its own rage, it must extend its influence until the laws of
nature themselves have been vanquished. Maldoror wants to
wield the power of life and death "even over the planets re-
volving in space." (271) That is why the "natural" need for sleep
is so humiliating to him. "Eaten with despair, he (must wallow)
in his own pain, until he has conquered nature." (298)

The episode with the female shark illustrates pointedly Maldoror's need for total power. At the beginning of the scene he
watches a ship in a storm as it begins to founder. A mere
spectator, he cries out, "Anyone who has not seen a ship lost in a
storm. . . . that person can never understand the accidents of
life." But as the disaster develops, the spectator becomes more
and more excited by the struggle against death which goes on
before his eyes:

> Oh God! how can a man live after experiencing so much ecstasy. It had
> just been granted me to witness the death agony of several of my fellow
> men. (206)

Progressively his emotions draw him into the scene. He is still a
spectator but he is no longer simply passive.

But soon nature itself will yield to Maldoror's desire for
action:

> The ship was too far away for me to hear distinctly all the moanings the
> wind swept my way; but I brought them closer by sheer will power.
> (207)

What he had been given to see he now gives himself to see,
abrogating a fact of nature by the strength of his will.

Maldoror's "participation" becomes increasingly intimate. Little by little, the "accident of nature" is made into his own work.

At last he takes the place of the storm itself, first with threats. "I felt that my hate and my words could leap through space, smashing the physical laws of sound...." The height of his power approaches, nature is prostrate before him, and his participation becomes total. He shoots a sailor trying to reach the shore. Now the shipwreck is his own work ("I was sure of their destruction"). The power of his will reaches its zenith when, no longer a spectator, he becomes the principal actor, leaping into the ocean to consummate his wildness by coupling with the female shark.

In this passage, Maldoror's rage for total power expresses the full range of its strategies, transforming the hero into a master spirit of nature itself.

Maldoror's hostility toward "nature" is matched by an even greater hostility toward men. "Misanthropy" is one of Lautréamont's ruling passions, and he rarely misses an occasion to vent his disgust for the human race. Many passages in *Maldoror* reach heights of apocalyptic joy, as the poet surveys the gay destruction of his *semblables*:

> If the earth were covered with lice, like grains of sand on the ocean shore, the human race would be annihilated in terrible agony. What a show! And me, with angel's wings, hovering in the air to watch it all. (190)

Scarcely an episode passes without some outburst of hate and rage, leaving us to wonder what humiliating wound had been suffered by Maldoror at the hands of men and their society.

We know that Narcissus-Maldoror is tormented by the face that most resembles his. For the "difference" is most cruel where the resemblance is strongest. Isidore Ducasse toys with his enemies and snares them in the trap of his imagination. But a young poet who has read Baudelaire, Sue, Maturin, and de Musset, who had spent years in the confinement of an imperial lycée, and lives in the indifference and isolation of a great city, knows without a doubt his most dangerous enemy is man, his *semblable*, and human society.

Aside from the apocalyptic scenes which have a flavor all their own, the episodes in which Maldoror confronts the world of men are surprisingly unvaried. In fact, two images of "society," the family and the prison, seem to exhaust Lautréamont's misanthropic rage.

I have already mentioned a number of episodes in which families are victimized by Maldoror's anger. Nor is it surprising that an adolescent poet, more or less abandoned by his father, having known no mother, should be haunted by images of family disaster. Even Maldoror's flamboyant adventure against God has the overtones of an aggrandized oedipal struggle.

The prison too is a fairly conventional image for the confinements of society. ("Man was born free, but everywhere he is in chains." Rousseau.) It is used over and over again in *Maldoror*, as in this scene which is often quoted:

> When a student is interned in a school, and governed for years . . . by a pariah of civilization whose eyes never leave him, he feels enormous waves of hate climb wildly into his brain like a thick smoke. . . . From the moment he had been thrown into this prison until the time, ever closer, when he leaves it, an intense fever turns his face yellow. . . .(152)[7]

This oversimplified notion of human situations recalls T. S. Eliot's phrase about Cyril Tourneur, another young but somber literary genius: "an intense, unique and horrible vision of life; but one which could impose itself, through limited experience, upon a very sensitive adolescent with a gift for words."[8]

But Maldoror and his "enemy" are not strangers to each other. They are accomplices in bitterness. Beyond the cruel "difference" beckons the elusive resemblance for which Lautréamont's hero longs. Although he "flees the human eye," although simply touching a member of the human race causes the "skin on his fingers to split open, like scales on a block of mica" (250), Maldoror is nonetheless fascinated by his *semblables*. When he launches his vindictive attack against the family, an incestuous dream mingles ith the violence, awakening, beyond all cruelty, Maldoror's nostalgia for a home. When he assaults an adolescent boy his erotic desire recalls once more the longing of Narcissus. In the midst of his most extravagant apocalypse Maldoror is

[7] See also: pp. 128, 167, 257, 280.

[8] T. S. Eliot, *Selected Essays,* Harcourt Brace, New York, 1950, p. 97.

haunted by his enemy: "two friends stubbornly trying to destroy each other, what a scene!" (252)

Indeed Lautréamont's misanthropy creates a dilemma for him. By destroying men, he destroys his own image, even if that image wounds him in its turn. "Each of them (Maldoror and man) recognizes in the other his own degradation" (252), but that is nonetheless an act of recognition.

Maldoror despises man and attacks him, for he has found the world nowhere more unbearable than among his *semblables*. But in destroying man it seems that he is destroying himself. To kill his image is already to kill himself a little, like those dogs who were mad for infinity and gorged themselves on their own blood. In pursuit of his vision Maldoror must "win a disastrous victory" against his *semblables* or "succumb." (252) Even victory is a disaster for the misanthrope.

The ambivalence of Lautréamont's poetic weaponry has already been described. In his battle against men the poet finds that he is betrayed by his own language, which recreates the destroyed values within the poem. He must then turn against the "human" form of his own words, which means turning against himself as well. In the same way, the hate which Lautréamont expresses for his *semblables* leads Maldoror to distrust the very resemblance he longs to establish, and to root it out at its source in his own nature. His flight from those parcels of the human form which he discovers in himself brings him to the verge of his most intimate violence, the strangeness and the failed exuberance of his metamorphoses.

The expression of Lautréamont's misanthropy in *Maldoror* scarcely needs to be detailed because the poem, in fact, bathes in it. Misanthropy creates an atmosphere into which the events of the poem are launched and which, in turn, acts on those events. Many of the episodes expressing Maldoror's hate for men do so en route to his other satanic exploits and will be discussed in other contexts. The metamorphoses in particular become one of the nodes of Lautréamont's narcissistic quest.

Before discussing the metamorphoses, however, it is important to locate the most visible of Maldoror's opponents, the "Great

Adversary" himself, whose presence occasions the poem's more frankly heroic episodes and triggers Maldoror's epic satanism. Lautréamont's hero finds an enemy worthy of him in the "clever bandit" whom he calls, according to his mood, the Great Everything, the All-Powerful, the Creator, the Eternal, etc. The struggle with God forces him not only to employ all the resources of subtlety and ruse but also to engage in heroic exploits of the wildest sort.

Two strategies predominate in Lautréamont's satanic warfare with God. In one Maldoror strikes in order to magnify his own strength. God becomes the Great Adversary whose sublimity exalts Maldoror to His own level. The satanic hero is strengthened by the blows he gives and receives, because God accepts him as an Enemy. In this sense Maldoror's satanism is a kind of ruse. By tricking the Adversary into accepting him as His equal, he becomes an exact but inverted image of the great power of the cosmos:

> Both of us live like neighboring kings, who know their respective forces, cannot conquer each other, and are weary of pointless battles. (216)

Because God has agreed to do battle, He enters into Maldoror's narcissistic quest. Instead of serving God, writes Maurice Blanchot, God serves Maldoror as "a fabulous mirror in which he sees, to the very depths of its horror, his own terrifying image."[9]

But God serves Maldoror in still another way. In the midst of the satanic struggle can be heard echoes of the "family" drama which lies at the heart of the narcissistic quest. Maldoror, the fallen angel, has disturbed the family harmony and the Creator, his "master," treats him as a "wayward son." (348) But the son's waywardness, as we have seen, consists in wanting to resemble his father. In this world of fantasy all the connections hold fast. The struggle with God and the quest for a resemblance engage, finally, the same passions. In either case, Maldoror wants to resemble his Father. Lautréamont's fascination with incest creates for itself a new language in his satanic struggle with the original of all "Ancestors."

But Maldoror's "revolt" goes deeper than that. Not only does

[9] *Lautréamont et Sade*, p. 121

he want to resemble his father; he wants to destroy the father's authority until he, the "wayward son," has become his father's father.

The satanic struggle is often accompanied by an undercurrent of maligning humor in which Maldoror attacks not so much God's power as his dignity. Maldoror threatens to make Him "whirl around like a top" (167), or to throw Him in a corner "like a bundle of string." (194) He sees Him sitting on a throne "made of human excrement and gold," where He rules "with idiot pride, His body wrapped in a shroud made of dirty hospital sheets." (182)

The satanic struggle raises Maldoror to the level of the All-Powerful. But at the same time it melts away the foundations of the divine power, turning the paternal dignity into ridicule. In the end it is the Father who resembles a wayward son, and the son who acts with dignity and generosity. Maldoror's satanism is most amply expressed in two episodes where this undermining strategy is much in evidence.

The first begins with an image of the Creator "stretched out on a road, His clothing torn. . . . Horribly drunk . . . He filled the air with incoherent words which I hesitate to repeat; if the supreme drunkard has no self-respect, I at least have to show respect for men." (235) One by one, the animals come to insult the Creator, until Maldoror, moved by this spectacle of a fallen God, arrives brimming with tolerance to defend Him:

> O men, you are terrible children; but I beg you, spare this great existence which has not yet slept off its filthy liquor. (236)

Fatherly and generous, Maldoror forgives the Creator for His bad behavior. He reverses the roles, and reigns morally over a God who has fallen into infancy.

The episode which follows this one describes the Creator's doubtful adventure in a house of ill-repute. The story (the longest in *Maldoror*) is charged with a fantastic eroticism which corrodes the paternal authority once and for all. This time God's moral collapse is irreversible. It shows even on His face, where "a drop of sperm (and) a drop of blood" have become lodged, stigmata of His descent among the passions. The fallen God wallows in His remorse like a lecher caught in the act by his own son:

> I thought I was the All-Powerful; but no. I have to hang my head and listen to remorse shouting at me: 'You're a miserable creature, that's all you are.' (247)

The Creator has descended "into the muddy labyrinth of the world," and Maldoror, His "wayward son," goes off, "making some quick reflections on the character of the Creator as a child." (237-49) The celestial father has been reduced into infancy by His son who, in exchange, has become the father himself.

But Lautréamont's satanism is not satisfied yet. Maldoror continues to pursue God until he discovers the last resting place of the Divine Spark in his own body. Assaulting God he finally must assault himself with the same destructive enthusiasm.

Maldoror now and then likes to take on a Promethean stance in his struggle against the Creator, declaring his desire to steal from God what belongs to man, in this case, not fire, but "consciousness":

> I'll whip your hollow carcass until I squeeze out of it those last bits of intelligence you tried to keep from man . . . as if you didn't know that sooner or later I'd find out where they were, and share them with my fellow men. (166)

Lautréamont knows that his best weapon in the satanic struggle is "intelligence," along with its ally, self-awareness (*conscience*). His Ode to Severe Mathematics (190-4) praises the powerful logic of theorems which the hero can use to "knock the Creator Himself from His pedestal made of human cowardice." Between Maldoror and his Adversary looms this invisible power which will give victory to the one who possesses it.

If we ignore the uncharacteristic generosity of Maldoror's Prometheanism—he describes it anyway as a ruse—there remains for us to consider the problem of *conscience* which lies at the heart of the struggle against God, as in this passage where Maldoror tells the origin of his implacable hatred:

> Know that I would rather feed hungrily on ocean plants from unknown

savage islands ... than know that you observe me, and reach into me consciousness with your sneering scalpel. (202)

At issue between Maldoror and God is *conscience*, a word whose ambiguities in French must be savored: consciousness, self-awareness, moral conscience. God observes the poet's secret life, and with his "scalpel" brings about the alterations which please Him. But Maldoror's *conscience* must be pure and inviolable if it is to illuminate the flow of his satanic will, as in the Ode to Severe Mathematics, where "the admirable methods of analysis, synthesis and deduction" form a weapon powerful enough to "spoil the terrible ruses of my mortal enemy." (193) Now he learns that the "weapon" of *conscience* has been secretly "poisoned" (194), that the work of the will bears the traces of an alien need against which he is powerless.

In the course of Maldoror's satanic struggle the All-Powerful floats above the clouds or descends to earth where He engages in extraordinary battle. But the cruelest of all His revelations takes place within the confines of the mind itself, where Maldoror's *conscience* turns against him, to become the instrument of another.

A bizarre episode illustrates the paradox of this double-edged *conscience*. Lautréamont tells the story of a somber pursuit, in which man tries desperately to outdistance the voice of his "moral conscience." But he finds that he is powerless to extinguish the voice of conscience without also extinguishing his intellectual consciousness. "He plunges his head up to the shoulders in the earthy complications of a hole," as if he knew that he had to blind the power of intelligence as well in order to be relieved of his moral suffering. But the solution doesn't work, because the energy of life reasserts itself. "The light reappears with its processional of rays, like a flight of curlews swooping down upon the lavender; and man ... once more is faced with himself." (214)

In the midst of the inextricable drama Maldoror appears to "defend man." He reveals that the Creator Himself is at the origin of moral conscience, since the day when Maldoror attacked him in the name of humanity and made him scream "terrible cries". "Those slithering, looped cries have sworn to be

the judges of human innocence." At the beginning of time
Maldoror's revolt had opened a wound in the consciousness of
man, and into the wound crept an alien principle, a failure of the
will ("conscience and its torments"), the presence of the All-
Powerful in the intimate reasoning of man.

Man continues to flee from the venom of his "moral conscience," until Maldoror decides to step in and take his place.
Now suddenly the roles are reversed. Maldoror pursues and
attacks the figure of conscience. He triumphs. But in the midst of
his triumph a change occurs. Maldoror's violence circles back
upon itself. He becomes strangely suicidal, as if all at once he
understood that "conscience and its torments" had nothing to do
with the allegorical figure he has just pursued and destroyed, but
lay instead in the secrecy of his own character. Maldoror's final
act is to lay his head under the blade of the guillotine, pursuing
his terrible adversary into this last refuge:

> Three times the blade raced along its groove with renewed vigor; three
> times my bodily carcass was shaken to its foundations, especially at the
> base of the neck. (218)

Maldoror repeats the desperate act of Man plunging his head
"into the earthy complications of a hole." But the hero's ambiva-
lent power asserts itself. The guillotine bounces off his neck,
unable to harm him; Maldoror too remains "face to face with
himself." His suicidal energy is turned aside, even death is powerless against him. But he cannot root out the pain of conscience
judging him from within. Unable even to die, he will be haunted
by his moral impotence. The secret enemy, who will eventually
destroy the very basis of his vision, is harbored within his own
being.

Maldoror discovers that his *conscience* obeys "another", that
the Great Exterior Object has slipped into the heart of his
experience. Narcissus cannot accept Rimbaud's *Je est un autre* (I
am another) which introduces ecstasy and self-abandonment into
the shape of his "identity." In Lautréamont's "whirlwind"
vision, anything foreign to the will, anything which does not
reflect the pure control of the center, must be crushed. God is
the Great Exterior Object. The natural universe is one sign of his

power, the poet's divided conscience is another. Maldoror's satanism now takes on a larger meaning. Whatever escapes the mirror
of the whirlwind, whatever stands firm in its outwardness is
embodied in the figure of God. For Narcissus, God is the ultimate tormentor:

> Oh! to see your intellect in the sacrilegious hands of a stranger. A
> heartless scalpel slashes deep into its underbrush. . . . Humiliation! our
> door is open to the savage curiosity of that Bandit up there. I never
> deserved this horrible torment, you hideous spy of my causality. If I
> exist, I am not another. I won't allow this equivocal plurality. I want to
> live alone in my secret understanding. Autonomy . . . or else change me
> into a hippopotamus. . . . My subjectivity and the Creator, that's too
> much for a single brain. (297)

Maldoror's satanism expresses a desperate desire for clarity. His
struggle with God is, ultimately, intellectual, because intelligence
for Lautréamont embodies the most profound violence of all.
Whatever is "known" has been made transparent. Intellect has
stolen its secrets. What Maldoror fears in God is His infinite
awareness, which can take him as an object and scrutinise him. In
the secrecy of his inward life Maldoror knows there is a force
which he cannot understand. What he had longed for was a world
in which his "subjectivity" would be the sole informing power,
but now he discovers a foreign presence at the very core of his
self-being. His struggle in *Maldoror* has only one goal, to exorcise
this foreign presence. That is why his "mind is scorched by a
condensed, always active reflectiveness." (295) Wielding the
power of his epic will, he struggles to shed light on the mysterious alien who has chosen to reside in the fibers of his intimate
self.

The inward and the outward enemies are seen, finally, to be
one. To strike a blow at God, Maldoror must strike off his own
head. The aggression becomes circular, and cannot be accomplished without returning to its source. The hero must struggle to
keep awake, to prevent the divine "scalpel" from operating
within him. For that reason, he has sworn "eternal hatred to the
boards of sleep." To stymie the All-Powerful he undergoes the
torments of insomnia. The outward threat has taken refuge in the
harbor of the self.

The parable of the wild dogs has already prepared us for this turn of events. They dream of a blind violence that will cease only when it has destroyed the root of their suffering, which is life itself.

It is significant that the grandiose battles between Maldoror and God take place for the most part in the first three cantos. But when the metamorphoses and other forms of concealed violence begin to operate, the heavenly Adversary loses his pre-eminence. It is as if Maldoror had discovered that the All-Powerful, of which he says, "I would like to love and adore you; but you are too powerful, and there is fear in my hymns," was, in fact, an element of his own being. At the beginning of the Fourth Canto, in any case, the fear has changed. Now Maldoror "fears nothing but his own self." (257)

IV

According to Pierre Reverdy, Lautréamont is the "integral destroyer" whose poetry is nothing but "furious rebuke."[10] For Camus, he is a "metaphysical dandy" motivated by the rage of total revolt."[11] The anger of Narcissus dissolves in a generalized violence from which nothing survives intact, not God, or man, or nature. The space of the poem is torn by Lautréamont's "whirlwind" violence until the center itself, Maldoror's violent will, disintegrates.

Lautréamont's hero has "denied father, mother, Providence, love, ideal, to think only of himself." (350) Maldoror is Narcissus. But even this stable center gives way under the weight of its destructiveness. When Maldoror strikes, the object slips out of reach and evaporates, only to reappear, intact, within the aggressor himself. The evil cannot be accomplished, in *Maldoror*, without returning to its source. Maurice Blanchot writes, "Maldoror cannot leave the evil to itself. . . . When he commits it, he withdraws with an irresistible movement which is like the evil flowing

[10] "Lautréamont n'a pas Cent Ans," *Cahiers du Sud* pp. 12-13.

[11] *l'Homme Revolté*, Paris, Gallimard, 1951, p. 109.

back upon itself, so that he experiences it in the double form of repentance and pleasure at harming himself." [12]

Behind this movement from evil to regret, from sadism to masochistic punishment, there is a logic which goes beyond the play of moral scruples. The repentance which causes Maldoror to return in tenderness to his victim is motivated, as much as the violence itself, by the quest for a resemblance. Maldoror punishes himself, but only because he longs to punish the fugitive "alien" he progressively discovers in the depths of his "identity." The logic of his struggle against nature, man and God, comes down to this struggle against himself which will end, apparently, only in his own destruction.

But at this paradoxical nadir of his adventure Lautréamont rediscovers the world of values. At the heart of the violence, as the narcissistic quest dissolves amidst the debris of the human world, it unexpectedly triumphs. If Lautréamont is a nihilist it is in Nietzsche's sense of the word, where to destroy means to "transvalue." Lautréamont the nihilist attacks the world of values to overturn and reverse them, replacing them not by "nothing" but by a world which is, at every point, contrary to the penitentiary reality against which he struggles.

We have seen that the object and source of the violence in *Maldoror* is the hero himself. His aggressive energies circle back upon him, to become an interior violence which intensifies as the poem develops. The progress of this interior violence constitutes the main adventure of Lautréamont's "transvaluation of all values." Maldoror "flees the human eye." To escape the failure of being "the son of man and woman," he will try to kill the human form in himself. After having dreamed of a holocaust that would annihilate the human race, Maldoror turns inward to obliterate the man he is, so that he can be reborn into another form, as an animal. It is the method of Lautréamont's metamorphoses.

This flight from humanity is the high road of *Maldoror*. The metamorphoses complete the violence committed by the hero by destroying the very image which he longed to imprint on all that surrounded him. In truth, what worse violence could there be for

[12] Blanchot, *Lautréamont et Sade*, p. 44.

Narcissus than no longer to resemble himself? Already, at the beginning of Canto IV, he asks anxiously, "Since when have I stopped resembling myself?" (251). Later this melting away of the familiar form will become the prelude to a new "identity." Narcissus will reclaim more than he loses.

Although they haunt even the early cantos of the poem, the animal transformations become more extravagant as the poem's "transvalued" space is progressively made over into an "image of the infinite." Lautréamont describes the meaning of this reversal for the first time in the Ode to Old Ocean.

The episode is composed of a series of comparisons between man and the ocean, which call to mind Baudelaire's sonnet, *l'Homme et la Mer*. In the power and harmony of the ocean the poet discovers an ensemble of qualities which are lacking in man. The result of these comparisons is to invoke a vast aquatic world which is the exact opposite of the world of man:

> Old ocean, your harmoniously spherical form . . . reminds me all too well of man's tiny eyes, which are like boar's eyes for smallness, and those of the nightbird for roundness of contour. . . .

> Old ocean . . . you never vary in any important respect, and if your waves are somewhere in fury, further off, in some other zone, they are completely calm. You are not like man . . . who is happy in the morning and irritable in the evening, who laughs today, cries tomorrow.

> Old ocean, the different kinds of fish nourished within you have not sworn friendship between them. Each species lives on its own. The varying temperaments and conformations in each of them explain perfectly what at first seems to be a mere anomaly. It's that way with man too, who doesn't have the same excuses. . . . From the highest to the lowest, each man lives like a savage in his den. . . . Another thing: the spectacle of your rich breasts calls forth the notion of ingratitude; because one thinks immediately of all those parents who meanly abandon the fruit of their miserable union. . . .

> Old ocean, you are so powerful, that men have learned it at their own expense . . . they can't master you, because they've found their master.

> Human majesty is borrowed, it doesn't impress me: but you, yes. (135-142)

Man is located on the side of impotence. Victimized by his

unstable emotions, he perpetually contradicts himself; he is the very opposite of all fecundity. The harmonious element of ocean overwhelms his poverty-stricken intellect. ("Men . . . have not yet been able . . . to measure your prodigious depths.") Ocean, on the other hand, belongs to the quality of grandeur. It never contradicts itself. The changes of Ocean compose an immoveable "identity" which is located beyond time. It embodies the purest element of fecundity. Yet, beyond these symmetrical differences, Ocean and Man are bound to each other because man is the slave, and the Ocean his master. The contraries are linked because each owes its very definition to the other.

The ocean is present to man in still another way. Its immense power undermines his humanity and is the source of a fearful discontent:

> Old ocean, your waters are bitter; they have exactly the same taste as those vile acids distilled by criticism upon the arts, the sciences, and everything. . . . Men must feel their imperfections strongly to criticize them that way! I salute you, old ocean. (138)

When man compares himself to the ocean, he becomes bitter, because he is forced to recognize his immense inferiority. Transported inward, the ocean becomes the measure of a perfection which he can never attain.

Marcel Jean and Arpad Mezai interpret the Ode to Old Ocean by substituting the word "Unconscious" for "ocean" whenever it occurs. [13] Between Man and the ocean, there exists the same relationship as between Man and "the whirlwind of his unconscious faculties." Their interpretation is seconded by a curious passage in the ode:

> I have often asked myself which it was easier to encompass: the depths of the ocean, or the depths of the human heart! . . . But let me say this: despite the ocean's awful depths, it simply can't compare . . . to the depths of the human heart. (138)

Thus the figure of Ocean serves to dramatize the dreadful spaciousness of the human heart. According to Lautréamont's ode

[13] *Maldoror*, Paris, Ed. du Pavois, 1947.

man is opposed to and drowned by what is deepest and most hidden in himself. The oceanic powers which "master" him are those of his own inwardness and Lautréamont concludes on a modern note: "Psychology still has a lot to learn."

Beyond the pure violence of his poem, Lautréamont's nihilism proposes another world, ruled by the values of the unconscious mind (the "human heart"), a world of natural plenitude in which man, unrepressed, uncivilized, and finally unhumanized, is liberated from all the prisons which he has secreted around him. Lautréamont carries Rousseau's famous watchword in the *Social Contract* to a remarkable extreme: man, for Lautréamont, cannot be free, cannot return to his birth and be reborn, until he has undone the sliest and most absolute of all the chains—the human form itself. The bitterness of old Ocean is the first solvent in *Maldoror* to loosen the hero's mooring as a "human" character.

Several pages further on, at the beginning of Canto II, Maldoror describes himself as a "vigorous defender" of morality, striding "firmly and unswervingly into the darkest corners and most secret fibers of the mind." (161) The complete anarchist turns out to be a moralist whose goal is to search out what is obscure in human nature, redefining man in terms of his own darkness. Already, in the Ode to Old Ocean, we see the moralist at work. "Old ocean, it is not absolutely impossible that you may hide in your depths some future usefulness for man." The ocean represents an ideal which ultimately will be man's hope. As in Hegel's parable, the slave must learn the skills of the master until he has become the master. Lautréamont's morality is simple, and wholly revolutionary. Man must give up resembling himself, so that he may embrace in his own life the infinite spaciousness of the ocean (the "human heart"). "I wish that human majesty embodied the reflection of your own."

The classical Narcissus wanted nothing in life except to love that one impossible presence on the surface of the water. In the same way, Lautréamont's Narcissus stands near the ocean, loving the self-image he discovers there. But unlike the traditional Narcissus, Maldoror does not see a reflection on the surface of the water; he sees the entire ocean as his reflected image, all the waters as the sign of his identity. In the ecstasy of discovering this vast reflection, Maldoror repudiates his other, older image, the one reflected back to him by his *semblables*. The waters appear before him, tempting him with a new existence which he longs for, and which is at the antipodes of the human world.

The ocean, for Lautréamont, represents the same primeval energy which it has never ceased to embody in the imagination of traditional cultures, the symbol of man's origin ("you remind me . . . of man's crude beginnings"), the domain of formless, precreated substance. In the words of Mircea Eliade:

> Matrix of all the possibilities of existence . . . water is the primordial substance out of which all forms arise, and to which they return, through regression or cataclysm. . . . Immersion in water symbolizes a return into the preformal, complete regeneration, a new birth. [14]

Lautréamont's "transvaluation of all values" requires the turbulence of the waters. The new morality of which Maldoror declares himself the vigorous defender is an oceanic morality, contrary in all things to any merely human ethic.

As the Ode to Old Ocean draws toward its close, Lautréamont's language becomes increasingly tense, the rhetoric is less balanced and harmonious. Until this point Maldoror's role has been that of an orator who vanishes behind the lyrical impetus of his words. But now he addresses himself to the ocean personally. "Ocean, answer me, do you want to be my brother?" He throws himself open to the waters, which suddenly lose their impassive grandeur, and become fraught with menace:

> Stir yourself wildly . . . more . . . still more, if you want me to compare you to the vengeance of God; stretch out your livid claws. . . .Unroll your terrifying waves, hideous ocean. . . . (142)

No more "crystal waves" and "harmoniously spherical form."

---

[14] *Traité de l'Histoire des Religions*, Paris, Payot, 1948, p. 168.

Now the ocean is hideous as divine vengeance, destructive as a beast with livid claws. Once more the violence of Lautréamont's "whirlwind" universe asserts itself, and Maldoror explains to us why this is so:

> Faced by your superior greatness, I would give you my love . . . if you didn't remind me so painfully of my fellow men . . . . I cannot love you, I hate you. (142)

Lautréamont dreamed he could transform the human world in favor of Old Ocean. But the master can never be free of his slave. To overturn the human world is still to preserve it in the form of its own negation. Maldoror "flees the human eye," but he discovers in the very plenitude of his new world the overturned image of those who resemble him. And this reminder unleashes the torrent of desperate energies which shape the poem.

The ocean is the element of love ("your friendly arms . . . open to caress my burning face"), it is the primordial image of Narcissus. But it is also the antipodes of the human world, and therefore an embodiment of purest evil. Maldoror asks joyously, but apprehensively:

> Tell me, are you the home of the prince of shadows? . . . Does Satan's breath create the storms that splash your salty waters to the clouds . . . I would rejoice to know that hell was so close to man. (142)

Once again we see the ambivalence of Lautréamont's vision. The waters express a world of positive values toward which Maldoror struggles, beyond his massive refusal of man and God. Water embodies the perfect reflection, the unconscious and unformed ground of all experience. But the ocean's plenitude, for Lautréamont, *is* by negation, by reversal, so that plenitude and negation become a single energy in *Maldoror*. To destroy and to wound becomes the only "affirmation" of which Maldoror is capable. The dark world of his imagination is the perfect, and opposite image of the formal world he hates.

What the Old Ocean expresses in a series of lyrical comparisons is present throughout *Maldoror*. The moral symmetry of the poem could be described in terms of a simple list of contraries:

Light	Darkness
man	animal
good	evil
form, artifice	formlessness, spontaneity
high, heights	low, depths
God	Satan (Maldoror)
land	water (blood, tears, etc)
cleanliness	filth, rot
sterility	fertility
light, day	night, obscurity
consciousness	the unconscious
slavery, chains, imprisonment	power, liberation

Already in the Ode to Old Ocean, the entire range of these contraries is present: the ocean is master, unfathomable, fertile, open to the depths; it is formless, embodies all the properties of the unconscious. The ocean is also the home of Satan; it has animal-like claws. Everywhere, the action of *Maldoror* takes place in this framework of oppositions; and almost always the presence of one or several of the terms implies all the others.

The satanic struggle opposes God and Satan (Maldoror). But the peripeteia of the struggle awaken all the possibilites of the dark realm: evil, filth, fecundity, water (or blood), darkness, animal nature.

In the apocalypse of lice, Filth, "Queen of empires," is greeted as a "heavenly liberator . . . invisible enemy of man." (188) Around the imagery of lice, filth and liberation, accumulates that of power, evil, fertility, darkness, satanism, liquidity (blood, ocean), which struggle against those of God, man, cleanliness, slavery, good, light, etc.

The experience of *Maldoror*, down to its smallest details, is organized according to this series of contraries. But Lautréamont's imagination prefers some terms of the series to others. The principal energy of the poem, for example, is expressed by the opposition between man and animal. A veritable "bestiary" inhabits the pages of the poem with a rollcall of zoological fantasies prefiguring Henri Michaux and Jorge Luis Borges. The encroachment of animal forms expresses the poem's final "transvaluation of values," its choice of the dark world against the world of man and light.

The role played by the metamorphoses is expressed clearly for the first time in the episode of the female shark. Refusing to seek his image among men, Maldoror discovers it in the depths of the ocean whose waters have been fertilized by blood. He encounters his "living portrait" for the first time in this female shark with whom he unites in a "long, chaste and hideous embrace." The interweaving of themes is dramatic: water and blood mingle to form an element of violence; Maldoror couples with a monstrous fish (symbol of fertility) which is also a murderous fish, the shark.

This episode illuminates others where the images of ocean, blood and fish are present. For example, one episode describes the Creator's feet plunged "in a vast pond of blood" from which "two or three prudent heads" peep out, half-suffocating. Here the water has become blood, and the men, "because they aren't fish" (182) are powerless against God's tyrannical whims. In another episode Maldoror boasts of having "lived for half a century in currents under the sea" (269), thereby explaining the origins of his power.

If water is the element of birth par excellence, then blood is a kind of negative water. The violence which wounds and bloodies is related to the powers of water and metamorphosis. That is why Maldoror is literally bathed in blood:

> Victories don't happen all by themselves. You've got to spill blood, lots of it, to create them and lay them at the feet of conquerors. Without those dead bodies and limbs you see scattered over the plain where the bloodbath wisely occurred, there would be no war, and without war, no victory. Do you understand? If you want to become famous, you've got to swim gracefully in rivers of blood. . . . (176)

In blood as in water, all things regress toward the original fecundity. The violence in *Maldoror* is the poet's answer to the advice he gives ironically to his reader: "Laugh, but cry at the same time. If you can't cry with your eyes, cry with your mouth.

You still can't do it? Then urinate; but I warn you, some liquid or other is necessary here. . . ." (256)

Everywhere the liquids multiply. To the blood and water are added tears, above all sperm, as God's sterile grandeur is decayed by "a drop of sperm (and) a drop of blood." (244)

The metamorphoses themselves are announced in the first sentence of Canto IV: "It is a man, or a stone or a tree that will start the fourth Canto." (250) After this, a strange impatience grips the objects of the poem. Almost every episode brings a new permutation in the human form. At the same time, the very space of *Maldoror* becomes fluid and changing. Objects melt into each other; language dissolves into a magma of unshaped words. Nothing remains stable in a world governed by the uncertainty of all forms:

> Two pillars, which it was not difficult and even less impossible to mistake for baobabs, appeared in the valley; they were taller than two needles. Actually, they were a couple of enormous towers. And, although two baobabs at first glance don't look at all like two needles, or even two towers, nonetheless, by skillfully managing the strings of prudence, one can state without fear of being wrong (because if this statement were accompanied by the slightest particle of fear, it would't be a statement; although a single word expresses these two phenomena of the soul which display characteristics different enough not to be lightly confused) that a baobab isn't so different from a pillar that comparison should be forbidden between these two architectural forms . . . or geometrical . . . or both . . . or neither . . . or rather massive, elevated forms. (252-3)

The rhetoric of the poem spreads like a net, engendering in its movement the alteration of all forms. The fairy-tale swiftness of the poem disappears, and a sort of logical-descriptive frenzy catches hold of the language, exposing a succession of changes which are like birthpangs:

> I am filthy. Lice gnaw at me. Pigs vomit when they see me. The pits and scars of leprosy form scales on my skin, which is bathed in yellow pus. I do not know the river's water, or dew from the clouds. On my neck as on a dung heap grows a huge mushroom with umbelliferous stem. Sitting on a shapeless chair, I haven't moved my limbs in four centuries. My feet have taken root in the ground; as high as my belly, they've become a sort of lively vegetation . . . which is not yet plant and no longer flesh. (264)

Each metamorphosis alters the human form a little more, transforming it into a succession of bizarre titans enlarged by the
interior ocean which has taken possession of them:

> I remember being terribly flattened against the belly of granite, while
> the tide rolled twice over this irreducible mixture of living flesh. (272)

In the next episode Maldoror wakes up dreaming that he is a
fabulous pig: "The day finally came when I was a pig! I tried out
my teeth on the bark of trees; I looked at the shape of my groin
with pleasure." (272)

But Maldoror's changes are not stable; as they impose themselves on the poem, each one resolves into the next. The next
episode describes still another strange creature: a web-footed sea
monster who lives in the ocean and its "crystal caves:"

> His long stay in the liquid element gradually brought about important
> changes in the human form . . . which my confused glances had enabled
> me to mistake . . . for a fish. (277)

Once more the waters give rise to that bodily transvaluation of
values, the fish, symbol of man's inclination toward "infinity."

The two preceding episodes illustrate the ambivalence of Lautréamont's metamorphoses. In one (where Maldoror dreams of
becoming a pig) the powers of evil predominate: "There wasn't
the slightest particle of divinity left in me. . . . When I wanted to,
I killed; it even happened pretty often, and nobody stopped me."
(273) But in the other episode, the violence has been transformed. The ocean and its sea creature embody a miraculous,
profoundly anarchic harmony. The satanic pig and the sea creature represent complementary aspects of the metamorphoses: on
the one hand, total liberation from the constraints of morality,
the ability to be and do pure harm; on the other hand, the
oceanic peacefulness of a world that has been wholly transvalued,
a place of pure fecundity. Yet even the ocean preserves the shape
of a negation. The sea creature tells how he flees the "rocky
continents," because when he nears land his miraculous powers
weaken: "He . . . wiped his eyes, which were bloodshot from the
awful constraint of approaching closely to dry land." (281) In
order for blood, that negative water, not to mix with the pure

waters of ocean, man and the world of dry land must remain distant.

We have by no means exhausted the variety of these metamorphoses which erupt in almost every episode of Cantos IV and V. But now, having grasped the "triumph" of Maldoror's flight toward the primeval image of Narcissus, we must remember that the triumph also contains a failure that will finally destroy Lautréamont's imaginary world. We have noticed the ambivalence of the poet's attitude toward the plenitude of Ocean: he loves it and tries, by all means possible, to embrace it; he hates it, because in the midst of plenitude he rediscovers the inverted image of his *semblables*. The ambivalence continues in the metamorphoses. In the episode of the satanic pig, for example, Maldoror can't decide whether his transformation is "the high and magnanimous result of perfect happiness," or, on the contrary, a "degradation" which is "probably a punishment inflicted on me by divine justice." (272). In any case, it appears that man continues to haunt him in his liberated form, because "Human laws still pursue [him] with their vengeance." (273) And this vengeance consists precisely in Maldoror's tormenting uncertainty. Are the metamorphoses a result of "perfect happiness" or are they a humiliation?

In the end it is Maldoror's dream of "perfect happiness" which fails. The metamorphoses attain the "image of infinity" which he has sought, but at the price of a strange suicide.

We can follow Maldoror's "fall" from episode to episode, as each transformation liberates him, only to scar him with the mark of a new failure. One thinks of Milton's conception of the fall of Satan in *Paradise Lost*. In both poems the reiterated choice of "evil" carries the hero progressively further from "heaven" (both Maldoror and Satan once belonged to Heaven's legions) and his original beauty in a series of adventures which scar that beauty until the final humiliation occurs: the "fallen angels" are transformed into beasts. For Maldoror, as for Satan, the last most humiliating change comes when God inflicts upon him the supremely symbolic form of the serpent.

Like Milton's hero, Maldoror cannot choose "evil" once and for all. Each episode in the poem forces him to reiterate his choice and to fall again. In his dream-struggle with the "silver-beaked lamp" he hesitates a moment before claiming victory: "For a moment he thinks he's been mistaken, and wonders if he ought to have followed the way of evil. . . ." (198) Each new adventure is also a new choice, and each choice brings about a further decline in the hero's original glory. After his victory over the divine messenger embodied in the lamp, Maldoror suffers the first defect in the splendor of his will: "He runs through the streets like a madman." (62)

Another important choice occurs in Canto III. For the first time, Maldoror enters into an animal form; he becomes an eagle in order to fight with an allegorical monster, the Dragon Hope. Here too, he emerges victorious from the battle, choosing against Hope, against the possibility of turning back. But his alter ego, Tremdall, who has watched the epic struggle from a distance, cries out to him: "You've got so many wounds, you can hardly stand upright on your feathery claws." (234) The fallen angel has lost his divine aspect; now he is wounded and stumbling with fatigue. Recall Satan's journey through Chaos, in *Paradise Lost*, where he is so battered by the cosmic storm that Milton compares him to a ship whose spars have been shattered and its sails torn. And yet, despite the rage of the storm, a vestige of former splendor remains; Satan, though battered, is still majestic. Maldoror too has been battered and transformed (bestialized), but into a creature which, despite its wounds, remains noble—the eagle.

Little by little, the evil extends its influence. Without listing all the forms of this encroaching "fall," which include the rotting king, the pig, the sea creature, the scarabee, etc., we can identify the end point of the fall in an episode where Maldoror is left finally with only his moral and physical decay, thereby consecrating the last failure of the metamorphoses:

Who is that? Who dares to drag the loops of his body close to my dark breast, like a conspirator? Whoever you may be, eccentric python, what excuse have you to pardon your ridiculous presence? Are you tormented by some vast remorse? Because you see, Boa, your savage splendor hasn't the mad pretension, I suppose, to escape the comparison I make between it and the traits of the criminal. (298-9)

Satan, his revolt crushed by God, was transformed into a
snake; that is how Milton conceived his punishment in *Paradise
Lost*. Maldoror's last adventure is also a punishment, finalizing
the violence which he has progressively turned against himself, by
a symbolic suicide. He threatens to destroy this serpent which is
the last embodiment of his own hunger for infinity: "crushing
the flight of your triangular head into the red grass, with a blow
of my heel" (299), he stamps out his own unrecognized image.

Lautréamont had forged his poem into a "whirlwind," with
himself at the eye of the storm. He longed to extend the sorcery
of his images, so that every point on the circle would reflect the
desire of Narcissus. But his violence finally shatters the fiction he
has built. In the course of his metamorphoses, Maldoror discovers
that the changes which erupt within him are so potent and so
uncontrollable that they must finally render him unknowable,
"eccentric," as he says of the mysterious serpent which is none
other than his own self.

Maldoror expresses the tragic contradiction of Narcissus trying
to discover his image amidst an ocean of shattered forms. The
image he discovers is no longer the same. It is unrecognizable,
even to himself. As the metamorphoses take possession of him,
Maldoror becomes obsessed with the failure to know his own
face. With his own hand, he marks the failure of his quest and the
inevitable end of his poem:

> There's only one thing left for me to do, and that is to break this mirror
> into pieces. . . . It's not the first time the nightmare of the momentary
> loss of memory has set up residence in my imagination . . . facing me
> with the ignorance of my own image! (271)

PART THREE:

Selected Passages from
Maldoror

I hope to God the reader turns as bold and momentarily ferocious as what he's reading; maybe then he'll find his way across the empty swamplands of these pages, which are dark, filled with poison. Unless he reads with a bold mind, and a clarity of thought at least equal to his distrust, the deadly spirits of this book will blot his soul up, as water blots up sugar. Not every one should read the pages that follow; only a few will taste this bitter fruit without danger. Therefore, timid soul, you'd better turn your steps back not forward before going any further into this unexplored country. Listen carefully to what I'm saying: turn your steps back not forward, like a son who respectfully lowers his eyes from the scrutiny of his mother's face; or else like an angle of chilly cranes lost in meditation; each winter, they fly powerfully across the silence, all sails extended, toward a certain point on the horizon, from which, all at once, a strange wind arises, forerunner of the storm. The oldest crane scouting out ahead, sees the wind and shakes his head like a reasonable person, which makes his beak shake too and click together. He's not very happy (I wouldn't be either if I were in his place). And his old featherless neck, dating back to three generations of cranes,

shakes up and down with irritation, as it sees the storm getting
closer and closer. He looks around with those experienced eyes
of his and then, prudently, before anyone else (because it's his
privilege to show his tail feathers to the other, less intelligent
cranes), he gives the watch cry of the lonely sentinel, to defeat
the common enemy. Flexibly shifting the point of the geometri-
cal figure (it may be a triangle, but one can't actually see the
third side formed in space by these strange migrating birds) either
to starboard or to larboard, like a good captain, he maneuvers
with wings that seem no bigger than a sparrow's, and takes
another, safer, philosophical road, because he's not stupid.

(Canto I, pp. 123-4.)

* * * * * *

All of my life I've seen narrow-shouldered men act stupidly all
the time. They oppress their brothers and degrade their souls in
all possible ways, calling the reason for their actions, glory. When
I saw this, I wanted to laugh like everyone else; but, strange
imitation, I couldn't do it. I took out a pocketknife with a single
sharp-edged blade, and cut myself at both corners of my lips. For
a minute, I thought I'd succeeded. I looked into the mirror at
this mouth which I had willfully mangled. But it was a mistake.
Besides, the blood flowing copiously from both incisions made it
impossible to say whether or not my smile was really the same as
that of other human beings. But after comparing for a few
minutes, I could see that my smile did not resemble the smile of
men; I mean, I wasn't laughing. . . .   *(Canto I, p. 126.)*

* * * * * *

. . . Not finding what I wanted, I raised my startled eyelids
higher, then higher still, until I saw a throne made of human
excrement and gold. Sitting upon it, imbecilically proud, his
body wrapped in a shroud of unwashed hospital sheets, was the
one who called himself the Creator. He held in his hand the trunk
of a rotting corpse, and carried it alternately from his eyes to his
nose, and from his nose to his mouth. You can guess what

happened when it reached his mouth. His feet were plunged in a vast lake of boiling blood, at whose surface two or three prudent heads appeared now and then, like tapeworms in the contents of a chamber pot, only to duck out of sight again with lightning speed: a healthy kick on the nose was usually the reward for a revolt against the rules, caused by the need to breathe another element. After all, those men weren't fish! Amphibians at best, they swam below the surface of the dreadful liquid . . . until the Creator's hand was empty. Then, with two large claws of his foot, like a pair of tongs, he seized another swimmer by the neck, and lifted him into the air over the reddish mud, exquisite sauce! He treated this one like the other. First he ate the head, the arms, the legs, then the body, until there was nothing left, because he munched the bones too. That's the way it went, for all the hours of his eternity. Sometimes he cried out: "I made you, so I can do what I want with you. Not that you ever did anything to deserve it, I won't deny that. I'm making you suffer, because I feel like it." Then he sat down again to his cruel dinner, moving his lower jaw which in turn moved his beard, filled with brains. O reader, doesn't this last detail make your mouth water? Not everyone can eat such good, fresh brains, caught only a few minutes ago in the *lake of fishes.* . . . *(Canto II, pp. 182-3.)*

* * * * * *

There is an insect which men feed at their expense, not because of any debt they owe, but because they are afraid of it. This insect doesn't like wine; it prefers blood, and if its legitimate needs were not satisfied, an occult power would cause it to grow as big as an elephant, and crush human beings like so many grains of wheat. You should see how it is respected—surrounded by doglike veneration, placed in high esteem above the animals of creation. It receives the head as a throne, fastening its claws with dignity at the roots of the hair. Later, when it is fat and old, imitating the custom of an ancient people, it is killed, so that it will not experience the debilities of old age. And then what a funeral it gets, like a hero! The bier which lofts it straight toward the cover of the tomb is borne upon the shoulders of the first citizens. Over the damp earth, freshly exposed by the grave-digger's wise spade, multicolored phrases are pronounced on the immortality of the soul, the emptiness of life, the inexplicable will of Providence, and the marble slab is lowered forever upon an existence filled with labor, which is now only a corpse. The crowd scatters, and night hurries to cover the walls of the cemetery with its shadow.

But console yourself for this painful loss, mankind! See its innumerable family advancing toward you; you have been gener-ously endowed, so your despair will be less painful, sweetened by the presence of these nasty abortions which later will become magnificent lice, incredibly beautiful, monsters with the appear-ance of philosophers. Several dozen precious eggs have been laid under its maternal wing, in your hair which has been sucked dry by these fearful strangers. The time is soon come for the eggs to hatch. Don't worry, born into this ephemeral life, the adolescent philosophers will grow up quickly. They'll grow and grow, until you feel them all right, with their claws and their suckers.

I suppose you're wondering why they don't devour the bones of your head, instead of simply drawing out your quintessential blood with their little pumps. Well, don't be impatient, I'm going to tell you: its because they're not strong enough. If their jaws were as vast as their infinite wishes, be sure that your brain, the retina of your eyes, your spinal column, your whole body would be used up; like a drop of water! Take a microscope, watch a louse at work on the head of a young beggar; it's something to see, believe me. Unfortunately, those bandits of the long hair are small. They wouldn't qualify for the draft, because they don't reach the size required by law. They belong to the lilliputian world of short thighs, and blind men classify them unhesitatingly among the infinitely small. I would pity a whale fighting with a louse. It would be devoured just like that, despite its size. Only its tail would be left, to spread the news. You can caress an elephant, a louse never! I advise you not to try anything quite that dangerous. If your hand is hairy, or even if it is made only of flesh and bone, watch out! That will be the end of your fingers; cracked open as in a torture machine. The skin will vanish, by some strange enchantment. Lice are incapable of doing all the evil they can think of. If you see a louse on the road, pass it by, don't lick the papilla of its tongue. You might have an accident. Things like that have happened. It doesn't matter, I'm already delighted with the quantities of harm it can do to you, O Human race; I only wish it could do more. . . .

O louse of the shrivelled eyeball, as long as rivers pour their watery slope into the depths of the sea; as long as stars circle in their orbit; as long as mute emptiness has no horizon; as long as humanity wounds its own flesh in fatal war; as long as heavenly justice hurls its thunders of vengeance on the egotistical earth; as long as man does not know his Creator, and mocks him, not without reason, mixing in a measure of disrespect as well, your reign over the universe will be assured, your dynasty will extend its encirclements from century to century. I salute you, rising sun, heavenly liberator, man's invisible enemy. . . .

As for me, if I am allowed to add some words to this hymn of praise, I'd like to say that I've built a ditch fifty miles square and proportionately deep. There, in its virgin filth, exists a living mine of lice. It fills the bottom of the ditch, snaking everywhere in veins of extreme density. Here is how I constructed this artificial mine. I plucked a female louse from the hair of humanity. I was seen making love to it three nights in a row, then I threw it into the ditch. For this once, human fecundation, which in other, similar cases would have failed, was accepted by fate; and after a few days, thousands of monsters began to see the light, swarming in a compact knot of matter. With time, this hideous knot became increasingly immense, acquiring the liquid properties of mercury as it ramified in different branches which feed by devouring themselves (their rate of birth is greater than their mortality) whenever I forget to throw down an infant bastard that some mother wants to get rid of, or an arm cut from a young girl at night, thanks to the effects of chloroform. Every fifteen years the generations of lice, feeding on man, diminish notably; this infallibly means that the time of their annihilation is close. Because man is more intelligent than his enemy, and manages to get the better of him. Then, with an infernal spade which increases my strength, I extract blocks of lice as big as mountains from the inexhaustible mine; I break them up with a hatchet, and carry them in the deep of night into the city streets. There they react to the heat of the human body, dissolving as on the first days of their creation in the tortuous galleries of the underground mine; they dig a bed in the gravel, and spread their trickling streams among the homes, like evil spirits. The guardian of the house barks, because it seems to him that a legion of unknown beings is penetrating the pores of the walls, bringing terror into the bed of sleep. Once in your life, you may have heard those long, painful howls. With helpless eyes he tries to pierce the obscurity of night; because his dog's brain is baffled. That humming sound irritates him, and he feels betrayed. Millions of enemies swoop down that way on every city, like clouds of grasshoppers. Enough for another fifteen years. They will struggle with man, causing him many painful wounds. And when the time is up, I'll send more. When I am breaking up the blocks of living matter, sometimes one fragment is denser than the others. Its atoms try angrily to separate from the mass and fly off to torment humanity; but the cohesiveness is tough, and it resists. In a supreme convulsion, they engender such an effort, that the stone, unable to scatter its living elements, is precipitated high into the air, as if it had been shot out of a gun; eventually it falls back again, plunging solidly into the earth. Sometimes a daydreaming farmer sees a meteor tear vertically through space, heading downward over the hill toward a cornfield. He doesn't know where the stone comes from. Now you have a clear and succinct explanation of the phenomenon.

If the earth were covered with lice like grains of sand on the ocean shore, mankind would be annihilated in terrible agony. What a show! And me with angel's wings hovering in the air to watch it all.   *(Canto II, pp. 185-194.)*

* * * * * *

I looked for a soul that resembled me, and couldn't find one. I searched all the corners of the earth; my perseverance was in vain. Yet I couldn't go on alone. I needed someone who shared my character, someone with the same ideas I had. It was morning; the sun came over the horizon in all its glory, when a young man rose into view, whose very presence strewed flowers where he walked. He approached me, and held out his hand, saying: "You have been looking for me, and now I come. Bless this happy day." But I answered: "Go away; I didn't ask for you; I don't need your friendship. . . ." It was evening; dark veils of night extended over nature. A beautiful woman cast her magic influence upon me: she looked at me compassionately, without daring to speak. I could barely make her out, and said: "Come closer, so I can see your face; at this distance the starlight isn't strong enough." With modesty, eyes lowered, she walked toward me over the grass. As soon as I could see her, I said: "I know that goodness and justice exist in your heart; we could never live together. At present you admire my beauty which has stricken more than one; but sooner or later you'd regret having given me your love; because you cannot know my soul. Not that I would ever be unfaithful: when someone gives themselves to me with such abandonment and confidence, I give myself to her with as much abandonment and confidence; but get this into your head, and don't forget it: wolves and lambs don't make sweet eyes at each other." What was it I needed, that I could reject with such disgust the best humanity had to offer? I simply didn't know! I wasn't yet in the habit of inspecting the phenomena of my mind, according to the best philosophical methods. I sat down on a rock near the sea. A ship had just piled on all its sails to get away from the coast. A vague dot appeared on the horizon: carried by the wind it came progressively closer, growing very quickly. The storm was about to start its assault; already the sky had darkened to a shade of black almost as hideous as the human heart. It was a large warship which now dropped all its anchors to keep from being swept against the rocky shore. The wind blew wildly from the four cardinal points, and tore the sails to ribbons. Blasts of thunder and lightning couldn't drown out the lamentations which came from the house without roots, the moving sepulcher. The surging masses of water hadn't yet snapped its anchor chains; but they had opened a breach in the side of the ship. A huge breach; because the pumps aren't strong enough to expel all those bundles of salty water tumbling and foaming over the bridge like mountains. The ship in distress shoots off cannon shots of alarm; but it sinks slowly . . . majestically. If you haven't seen a ship sink in a storm, amidst flashes of lightning, in deepest darkness, while its crew is overwhelmed by a despair you can understand, then you have not experienced the accidents of life. At last a cry of wild pain arises from the ship, as the ocean redoubles its awful assault. It is the shriek of human strength abandoning hope. Each sailor is cloaked in resignation, giving over his fate into the hands of God. They huddle like a flock of sheep. The ship in distress shoots off cannon shots of alarm; but it sinks slowly . . . majestically. The pumps have been going all day, but it's no use. Night falls, relentless and thick, crowning this gracious spectacle. Each sailor thinks that once he is in the water, he won't be able to breathe; because as far back as he can remember there are no fish in his family. But he is determined to hold his breath as long as he can, prolonging his life by two or three seconds; that is the avenging irony he wants to flaunt in death's face. . . . The ship in distress shoots off cannon shots of alarm; but it sinks slowly . . . majestically. They don't know that the sinking ship is causing a whirlpool; that mud from the sea bottom has mixed in with the troubled waters; a force from below, reacting to the tempest above, has stirred the water into jerky, nervous spasms. So no matter how cool and collected he is prepared to be, the future drowned man, if he thought it out a bit more realistically, would consider himself lucky to prolong his life in those whirlpools of the abyss, by half of an ordinary breath, for good measure. So he won't get a chance to thumb his nose at death, his fondest wish. The ship in distress shoots off cannon shots of alarm; but it sinks slowly . . . majestically. No, that's wrong. There are no more cannon shots; it's not sinking anymore. The nutshell has gone completely under. Oh God, how can a man live after experiencing so much ecstasy? It had just been granted me to witness the death agony of several of my fellow men. Minute by minute, I followed the episodes of their anguish. Sometimes an old woman barking with fear was tops on the market. Sometimes the shriek of a tiny baby drowned out the officer's commands. The ship was too far away for me to hear distinctly all the moanings the wind swept my way; but I brought them closer by sheer will power, and the optical illusion was complete. Every quarter of an hour, when a stronger gust of wind wrenched the ship in great lengthwise cracks, and the deadly sounds blew toward me amidst the cry of the seagulls, increasing the shrieks of those who would be offered up in a holocaust to death, I jabbed a piece of sharp iron into my cheek, and thought secretly: "They're suffering more." That way, at least, I had a point of comparison. I yelled, I screamed threats at them from the shore, certain they could hear me. I felt that my hate and my words could leap through space, smashing the physical laws of sound, to reach those ears half-deafened by the roaring of the angry sea. I wanted them to know about me, and to exhale their revenge in fits of impotent rage! Now and then I looked toward the cities which slept on dry land; no one was aware that a ship was sinking a few miles from shore, with a crown of flesh-eating birds, and a pedestal of undersea giants whose stomachs were empty; that cheered me up, I felt hopeful again. I was sure now they wouldn't get away! But just in case, I brought along my double-barreled rifle. If one of those sailors tried to swim ashore, a bullet in the shoulder would break his arm, and that would be that. At the height of the storm, I noticed a head stroking desperately over the waves, its hair thrown wildly about. The man had swallowed quarts of water by now, he sank into the depths like a piece of cork; but then he was on the surface again. As he looked toward the shore, he seemed to defy death. His presence of mind was marvelous. A bloody wound made by the point of some reef had gashed his noble face. I could see the peach fuzz on his upper lip, when lightning flashes lit up the darkness. He couldn't have been more than sixteen years old. Now he was about two hundred yards from the cliff. I looked down at him easily! What courage, what spirit! His head seemed to mock destiny, as he swam through the waves which parted reluctantly before him! . . . My mind was already made up. I had to keep my promise, I owed it to myself: the final hour had sounded for all, not one of them could escape. That was my decision; nothing would change it. . . . A sharp report was heard, and the head sank, never to reappear. This

murder didn't give me as much pleasure as you might think,
because I was tired of killing all the time. It was a habit by now,
something I did because I couldn't help it, but it gave me only a
small thrill. The senses coarsen and blur. What pleasure could I
take in the death of this human being, when over a hundred more
were going to be offered to me in their struggle against the waves,
when the ship finally went under? There wasn't even any danger
in causing this death; because human justice slept a few feet away
in the houses, rocked by the winds of that awful night. Now that
years weigh heavily on my body, let me announce this solemn
truth in all earnestness: I wasn't as cruel as it came to be told
among men; but sometimes their evil deeds ravaged me year after
year. Then my wildness would break out uncontrollably; I fell
into fits of cruelty, and became deadly for anyone of my race
who approached my haggard eyes. If it was a horse or a dog, I let
it pass: did you hear what I said? Unfortunately the night of that
storm, I was in one of my rages, my reason was overpowered
(because usually I was just as cruel, but more careful); anything
that fell into my hands had to perish; I won't try to make
excuses for my errors. It's not all the fault of my fellow men. I'm
telling the simple truth, while I wait around for Judgment Day,
which makes me scratch the base of my neck in advance. . . .
What do I care about Judgment Day! I never lose control, I was
just saying that to fool you. When I commit a crime, I know
what I'm doing: I didn't want to do anything else! I stood on the
rock, while the wind swirled in my hair and tore at my cloak. I
was in ecstasy, watching the power of the storm sweep against
the ship, under a starless sky. I followed all the episodes of the
drama in triumph, from the time the ship dropped anchor, to
when it was sucked under like a deadly coat, dragging down into
the bowels of the sea all those who wore it wrapped around
them. But the time approached when I myself would become an
actor in these wild scenes of nature. The place where the ship had
struggled against the storm revealed that it had gone down to
spend the rest of its days on the ground floor of the sea, but
some of the men were thrown clear by the waves and reappeared
at the surface. They held on to each other two by two, and three
by three; that wasn't the way to save their lives, because their

movements got all tangled up, and they sank like broken pitchers. . . . What's that army of sea monsters speeding in this direction? Six of them. Their fins slice through the leaping waves. The sharks have soon turned all those human beings waving their limbs in the unsteady continent, into an omelette without eggs, which they share between them according to the law of the strongest. Blood mingles with the water, and water mingles with the blood. Their ferocious eyes shed plenty of light over the scene of the bloodbath. . . . But what's that commotion over there in the water, near the horizon? It looks like a tornado. What incredible strokes! Now I see what it is. A huge female shark, come to get its share of the chopped duck liver and have some cold soup. She's furious, because she's hungry. A fight starts between her and the other sharks, over the few palpitating limbs still floating here and there, without a word, in the red cream. To the right and to the left, her teeth dish out fatal wounds. But three live sharks still surround her, and she has to swing around in all directions to neutralize their attacks. With an increasing emotion he has never felt before, the observer on the shore watches this new type of naval battle. He keeps his eyes on the brave female shark whose teeth are so strong. He no longer hesitates; he aims his rifle and, with his usual skill, hits one of the sharks in the ear with his second bullet. Now two sharks are left, but their fury is all the greater. From high on his rock the man with bloody saliva leaps into the sea and swims toward the pleasantly colored rug, holding in his hand the steel knife which never leaves him. Now, each shark has an enemy. Closing with his tired opponent, he takes his time plunging his blade into the shark's belly. The moving citadel easily gets rid of its last adversary. . . . Now they are face to face, the female shark and the swimmer who has saved her life. They looked into each other's eyes for a few minutes, each one surprised to find the other's gaze so fierce. They swim in a circle, eyeing each other and thinking: "I was wrong before now; this one is even worse." Then, with one movement, they slipped closer under the water, filled with mutual admiration, the female shark stroking with her fins, Maldoror beating with his arms; as they held their breath, each one felt profound veneration for the other and longed to contemplate his own living portrait for the first time. When they were three yards apart they fell effortlessly against each other, like two lovers, embracing with dignity and gratitude, in a hug as tender as that of a brother and sister. Carnal desires followed quickly upon this show of friendship. Two nervous thighs clung tightly to the monster's viscous skin, like two leeches; arms and fins enlaced tenderly around the loved one's body. Soon their breasts and throats were mingled in a sticky mass, smelling of seaweed; engulfed by the onblowing storm; in the flicker of lightning; their bridal bed made of the foaming waves, carried as in a cradle by underwater currents, rolling over and over into the unknown depths of the abyss, they came together in a long, chaste and hideous act of love. . . . At last I had found someone who resembled me! . . . From now on I wasn't alone in life! . . . She had the same ideas I had! . . . I was face to face with my first love!   *(Canto II, pp. 203-211.)*

*   *   *   *   *   *

There are hours in his life when a man stares wildly at the green membranes of space, his hair thick with lice; for he seems to hear the ironic laughter of a ghost somewhere before him. He stumbles and lowers his head; what he has heard is the voice of conscience. He runs from the house with the speed of a madman, devouring the rugged plains of the countryside in the first direc- · tion his stupor indicates. But the yellow ghost does not lose sight of him and pursues with equal speed. Sometimes on a stormy night, legions of winged squid can be seen above the clouds; from a distance they look like flocks of crows, powerfully winging their way toward the cities of men, with orders to warn them to change their ways. Meanwhile the stone's dark eye sees two creatures pass in a flash of lightning, one behind the other. Wiping a tear of compassion from its chilled eyelids, it cries out: "There's no doubt he deserves it; it's only justice." Having spoken, the stone resumes its ferocious quietness. With a nervous shudder it watches the manhunt, and the great lips of the shadow vagina from which huge spermatozoa flow like a river, before taking flight in the ghastly ether. Their wingbeats shadow all of nature, and the solitary legions of squid saddened at the sight of those dark, inexplicable flashes. Meanwhile, the steeplechase goes on between the two tireless runners, and the ghost breathes torrents of fire out of his mouth onto the back of the human antelope. If while accomplishing his duty, the ghost should meet up with pity trying to block his way, he gives in disgustedly to its prayers, and lets man get away. The ghost clucks his tongue, as if he were telling himself to give up the pursuit, and go back to his kennel until the next time he is called. His criminal's voice can be heard in the deepest layers of space; and when his awful howling penetrates the human heart, man, they say, would rather have death for a mother than remorse for a son. He plunges his head up to the shoulders in the earthy complications of a hole; but conscience dissolves that ostrich ruse. The hole evaporates, drop of ether; light reappears with its processional of rays, like a flight of curlews swooping down upon the lavender; and man, eyes pale and open, once more is face to face with himself. I have seen him head for the seacoast, climb a promontory battered, beaten by crests of foam, and leap like an arrow into the waves. Here is the miracle: the next day the corpse reappeared on the surface of the water which had carried its ruined flesh toward the shore. Man crept out of the mold his body had made in the sand, wrung the water from his soaked hair, and started once again along the road of life, his face downcast and mute. Conscience judges our thoughts and our most secret acts severely, and is never wrong. Since it can rarely prevent the evil, conscience is always tracking man like a fox, especially at night. Avenging eyes, which ignorant science calls *meteors*, spread their livid flame as they roll over and over, pronouncing words of mystery . . . which man understands! Then his bedside shudders with nervous spasms, crushed by the weight of his insomnia, and he hears the sinister breathing of the vague noises of night. Even the angel of sleep gives way: it climbs back to heaven, wounded fatally in the head by an unidentified stone. All right, I'm offering to defend man this time; me, despiser of all virtues; me, unable to forget the Creator since that glorious day when I pulled the annals of heaven from their pedestal, where by some devilish trick *his* power and *his* eternity had been inscribed; I applied the suckers of my four hundred octopus arms to his armpit, and made him cry out horribly. . . . Those cries became vipers, sliding out of his mouth to hide in the bushes, near ruined walls, watching by day, watching by night. Those slithering, looped cries with their small flat heads and treacherous eyes, have sworn to be the judges of human innocence. When human innocence strays in the wilderness, on the far slope of hills, along the crest of sand dunes, it is pretty quick to have a change of heart. Unless it's already too late; because sometimes man can see the poison enter the veins of his leg, through an almost invisible puncture before he has had time to retrace his steps, and go another way. And so the Creator shows remarkable self-control, even in the midst of horrible suffering; he knows how to draw from their own breasts germs which are harmful to the inhabitants of the earth. He must have been awfully surprised to see Maldoror, changed into an octopus, advancing against his body with eight monstrous paws, any one of which could easily have wrapped itself around a planet like a powerful lanyard. Taken unawares, he struggled for a while against that viscous hug which got tighter and tighter. . . . I was worried about some underhanded trick on his part; so after I had dined amply on the globules of his sacred blood, I let go of his majestic body and went to hide in a cave which has been my home ever since. He searched everywhere, but couldn't find me. That was a long time ago; by now I think he knows where I am. He's careful to leave me in peace; the two of us live like neighboring kings, each of whom knows the other's strength, cannot vanquish him and is tired of the useless battles of the past. I'm afraid of him, he's afraid of me; each of us, without being beaten, has felt the heavy hand of his adversary, and we leave it at that. Although I'm ready to start up again, any time he wants to. But he'd better not wait for an unguarded moment to set his hidden plans into motion. I always keep an eye on him. And he'd better not send conscience and its torments down onto the earth. Because I've taught men how to use weapons that will give them the advantage. They're not too good at it yet; but, you know, as far as I'm concerned, conscience is like straw in the wind, that's all. If I wanted to use the present occasion to complicate these poetic arguments, I would add that I care more for the straw than for conscience; at least straw can be useful to a hungry cow, but all conscience can do is show its steely claws. They met up with a painful failure, the day they stood before me. Since conscience had been sent down by the Creator, I thought it best not to let her get in my way. If she had displayed the modesty and humility proper to her position, which she should never have abandoned, I might have listened to what she said. But I didn't like her arrogance. I stretched out one hand and crushed her claws with my fingers; they turned to dust under the growing pressure of this new style mortar. I stretched out the other hand and yanked her head off. Then I chased that woman out of my house with a whip and never saw her again. I kept her head as a souvenir of my victory.... A head in my hand, gnawing its skull, I stood on one foot like a heron, at the edge of a cliff slashed in the mountainside. They saw me descending into the valley, while the skin of my chest was motionless, calm as the lid of a tomb! With a head in my hand, gnawing its skull, I swam the most dangerous depths, along deadly reefs, and dived beneath the deepest currents where I observed the struggles of seagoing monsters; I swam away from shore, until my strong eyes could no longer see back to it. Hideous cramps shuddered near my limbs with paralyzing magnetism, but they were afraid to come any closer as I vigorously cleaved the waves. They saw me returning to the beach, perfectly healthy, while the skin of my chest was motionless, calm as the lid of a tomb. A head in my hand, gnawing its skull, I climbed the stairs of a high tower. I reached the dizzy platform, my legs weary. I looked around at the countryside, at the sea; I looked at the sun and sky. With the use of my feet I pushed away the granite, which held firm, as I defied death and divine vengeance in a supreme mockery, diving like a stone into the mouth of space. Men heard a painful thud when the ground met up with the head of conscience which I had abandoned in my fall. They saw me descending with the slowness of a bird borne up by an invisible cloud; I picked up the head, forcing it to witness the triple crime I was going to commit that very day, while the skin of my chest was motionless, calm as the lid of a tomb! A head in my hand, gnawing its skull, I walked toward the square where the guillotine rose up. I lay the suave

grace of the necks of three young girls under the blade. Executioner of high works, I released the cord with the obvious skill of
a lifetime; and the triangular-shaped blade slid obliquely down,
slicing off three heads which looked sweetly up at me. Then I
placed my own head under the ponderous razor blade, and the
executioner got ready to perform his duty. Three times the blade
raced along its groove with renewed vigor; three times my bodily
carcass was shaken to its foundation, especially at the base of the
neck; as when you dream you are crushed by a collapsing
building. The crowd was so stupefied, it let me go by, as I hurried
away from the funerary square. They saw me opening my way
through its undulating waves with my elbows; walking, full of
life, straight before me, head high, while the skin of my chest was
motionless, calm as the lid of a tomb! I told you I wanted to
defend man this time; but I'm afraid my apology doesn't really
express the truth; so, I'd better keep my mouth shut. Humanity
will gratefully applaud this decision.   *(Canto II, 213-218.)*

*   *   *   *   *   *

Remember the names of those angelic imaginary beings which
my pen extracted from my brain during the second Canto,
shining with a glow from within themselves. They died as they
were born, like sparks whose rapid extinction the eye can barely
follow on the burnt paper. Leman! . . . Lohengrin! . . . Lom-
bano! . . . Holzer! . . . for a moment you appeared on my
charmed horizon, filled with youth; but I let you fall back into
chaos, like diving bells; you will never come out again. Just
remembering you is enough for me now; you've got to leave
room for other substances created by the stormy flow of a love
which has sworn never to slake its thirst among the human race.
A hungering love that would devour itself, if it couldn't seek
nourishment in the realm of heavenly fictions: creating at last a
pyramid of angels more numerous than insects swarming in a
drop of water, it will weave them together into an ellipse and
whirl them around it. During this time a traveler, brought to a
standstill near a great cataract, will see in the distance, if he lifts
his eyes, a human being carried toward the cave of hell by a

garland of living camellias! But . . . quiet! the image of the fifth ideal appears gradually on the misty screen of my intelligence, like the hovering folds of an aurora borealis. . . . Mario and I rode along the shore. Our horses stretched out their necks and pierced the membranes of space, tearing sparks from the flat stones along the beach. The cold wind blew in our faces; it billowed through our cloaks and tousled the twin manes of our horses. A seagull shrieked and fluttered its wings, trying vainly to warn us that a storm might be near; it cried out: "Where are they galloping so wildly?" We said nothing, plunged in reverie, letting the mad race carry us where it would. The fisherman saw us pass, with the speed of an albatross, and thought he saw running before him the *two mysterious brothers*, as they had been called, because they were always together. Hurriedly he made a sign of the cross and hid with his paralyzed dog under a deep rock. The inhabitants of the coast had heard strange stories about these two characters, who appeared on the earth, amidst the clouds, during periods of calamity, when a horrible war threatened to plunge its harpoon into the breast of two enemy countries, or when cholera prepared to hurl rot and death into whole cities with its slingshot. The oldest looters of wrecked ships frowned, claiming that the two phantoms whose vast black wings everyone had seen during hurricanes, over sandbanks and reefs, were the spirit of the earth and the spirit of the sea. They rode their majesty through the air during great revolutions of nature, linked together by an eternal friendship whose rarity and glory had awakened the astonishment of the indefinite cable of generations. Flying side by side, like two condors of the Andes, it was said they liked to float in concentric circles in the high layers of atmosphere near the sun; that they fed, in those regions, on the purest essences of light, deciding only with reluctance to lower their vertical flight toward the stricken orbit where the globe of man revolved deliriously, inhabited by cruel spirits who massacred each other on the field of battle (when they weren't killing treacherously, in secret, in the heart of cities, with the knives of hate or ambition), feeding on creatures who are as full of life as they are but are placed a few degrees lower on the chain of existences. Or else they resolved to awaken repentance in man with their prophetic songs,

stroking powerfully toward the sidereal regions of a planet re-
volving in thick emanations of pride, sneers and insult which
arose like pestilential vapors from its ugly surface; it seemed as
tiny as a ball, almost invisible because of the distance. There were
always times when they bitterly regretted their good will; unrecognized, pursued by insults, they hid deep inside volcanoes,
conversing with the wild fire seething in cauldrons underground;
or else in the depths of the sea, to soothe their disillusioned eyes
among the most ferocious monsters of the abyss, which to them
seemed models of sweetness, compared to the bastards of humanity. When the darkness of night fell, they flung out of the
porphyry craters and the currents undersea; they left far behind
them the rocky chamber pot where the constipated anus of all
those human cockatoos ran loose. Soon they could no longer
make out the silhouette of that disgusting planet. Then, saddened
by their failed attempt, among stars which sympathized with
their pain, beneath the eye of God, the angel of earth and the
angel of the sea embraced and wept. . . . *(Canto III, pp. 220-223.)*

* * * * * *

It was a spring day. Birds twittered their canticles, and men
accomplished their tasks in the saintliness of fatigue. Everything
labored at its destiny: trees, planets, sharks. Everything, except
the Creator! He was stretched out on a road, his clothing torn.
His lower lip hung down like a sleepy cable; his teeth weren't
brushed, and the blond curls of his hair were covered with dust.
His body had fallen wearily against the stones, and tried hope-
lessly to get up. But his strength had left him; he lay there, weak
as an earthworm, unfeeling as the bark of a tree. The path was
rutted by his wildly jerking shoulders; and streams of wine filled
all the ruts. The pig-crotch of stupor covered him with its
protective wings, watching him with lover's eyes. His legs swept
the ground like two blind masts, their muscles completely un-
strung. Blood flowed from his nostrils: when he fell his face had
knocked against a pole. He was drunk! Horribly drunk! Drunk as
a bedbug which has sucked up three barrels of blood in a single
night! He filled the air with incoherent words which I hesitate to

repeat; if the supreme drunkard has no self-respect, I at least have
to show respect for men. Did you know that the Creator . . . was
a drunkard? Have pity on that lip soiled in the cups of orgy! The
hedgehog passing by shook its quills into his back, and said:
"That's what you get. The sun is halfway across the sky: get to
work, you bum, and stop eating other people's bread. Wait a
minute, see if I don't call the cockatoo with its hooked beak."
The woodpecker and the owl, passing by, drove their beaks into
his belly, and said: "That's what you get. What are you doing
down here on earth? Is it to make such a ghastly spectacle of
yourself to the animals? But the mole, the cassowary, or the
flamingo haven't got the slightest intention of imitating you, I
swear it." The donkey, passing by, gave him a kick in the head,
and said: "That's what you get. What did I ever do to you, to
deserve such long ears? Everyone makes fun of me, even the
small crickets." The toad, passing by, spat in his face and said:
"That's what you get. If you hadn't given me such huge eyes, and
I had found you this way, I would have chastely hidden the
beauty of your limbs under a rain of crowfoot, forget-me-nots,
and camellia blossoms, so that no one would have seen you." The
lion passing by, bowed his regal head and said: "As for me, I
respect him although his glory seems eclipsed for the moment.
The rest of you are too proud, and you're cowards as well,
attacking him when he was asleep. How would you feel if you
were in his place and had to put up with all the insults you've
been showering on him?" Man, passing by, stopped when he saw
the Creator so misunderstood; to the applause of the crab-louse
and the viper, he shit on his royal face for three days! Shame on
man for that insult; he has not respected the enemy, collapsed in
the mixture of mud, wine and blood; defenseless, almost inani-
mate! . . . Finally the sovereign God was awakened by all those
petty insults; he did his best to get up, and stumble over to a
stone where he sat; his arms hanging down like the testicles of a
dying tubercular, he stared glassily, coldly over all of nature,
which belonged to him. O men, you are terrible children; but I
beg you, spare this great existence which has not yet slept off its
filthy liquor; he's not strong enough to sit up yet, collapsing
heavily onto the rock where he was seated, like a traveler. Watch

this beggar passing by; he saw the dervish hold out a hungry arm. Without knowing who the object of his charity was, he dropped a piece of bread into that hand which begged for pity. The Creator expressed his gratitude, with a shake of his head. Oh, you'll never know how hard it is to hold the reins of the universe in your hands all the time! The blood rushes to your head, when you concentrate on creating one last comet out of nothingness, with a new race of spirits on it. When the mind has been shaken so profoundly from top to bottom, it shrinks away like a victim; once in a lifetime, it can even fall into the errors you have just witnessed.   *(Canto III, pp. 235-237.)*

*   *   *   *   *   *

A man or a stone or a tree is going to begin the Fourth Canto. When your foot slips on a frog, you get a feeling of disgust; but when you even brush your hand against the human body, the skin cracks on your fingers like scales chipped from a block of mica when you hit it with a hammer. Just as the heart of a shark goes on beating stubbornly on the deck, even an hour after it is dead, so our entrails keep on shuddering long after the touch. That's the amount of horror man feels for his fellow man! Maybe I'm wrong in saying that; but then again, maybe I'm telling the truth. I know, I can conceive an illness more terrible than eyes swollen by long meditations on the strange character of man: but I'm still looking . . . and I haven't been able to find it. I don't think I'm less intelligent than the next person, and yet who would dare to claim that my investigations have been a success? What a lie would be spoken by his mouth! The ancient temple of Dendarah is located an hour and a half from the left bank of the Nile. Today, incredible swarms of wasps have taken over its gutters and cornices, hovering among the columns like waves of thick black hair. They are the only inhabitants of the cold portico, and they guard the entry to the halls as if it were an hereditary task. I compare the buzz of their metallic wings to the endless clashing of icebergs hurled against each other in the fury of the polar seas. But if I consider who is sitting on the throne of the world, by the will of providence, and if I consider the things he does, the triple wings of my suffering make a much louder sound! When a comet appears suddenly in some part of the sky, after having been absent for eighty years, it shows its vaporous, gleaming tail to the inhabitants of earth, and to the crickets, who are probably unaware of the distance it has travelled. It's not the same with me. When my head is cradled in my hands as I lie in bed, the jagged shapes of a thirsty, mournful horizon flash across the depths of my soul, and I abandon my thoughts to dreams of compassion, blushing for man! Doubled over by a freezing wind, the sailor hurries back to his hammock after having stood his watch: why can't I receive the same consolation? The idea hammers through me like a forged nail, that I have willingly fallen lower than my fellow men, and so have less right than others to complain about our destiny, locked on the frozen crust of the planet, or about the essence of our perverted souls. Explosions of coal gas have been known to annihilate whole families; but their agony was short, death is almost sudden amidst the wreckage and the harmful gases: as for me. . . . I still exist like basalt. . . . *(Canto IV, pp. 250-251.)*

* * * * * *

I am filthy. Lice gnaw at me. Pigs vomit when they see me. The pits and scars of leprosy cover my skin, which is bathed in yellow pus. I do not know the river's water, or dew from the clouds. On my neck, as on a dung heap, grows a huge mushroom with umbelliferous stem. Sitting on a shapeless chair, I haven't moved my limbs in four centuries. My feet have taken root in the ground; as high as my belly they've become a sort of lively vegetation which is not yet plant but no longer flesh; it is filled with disgusting parasites. And yet my heart beats. How could it beat if the rot and emanations from my corpse (how can I say body?) didn't nourish it abundantly? Within my left armpit a family of toads has taken up residence, when they move it tickles me. Be careful that one of them doesn't escape, and scratch the inside of your ear with its mouth: it would be capable afterward of sneaking into your brain. Within my right armpit lives a chameleon, always ready to ambush the toads, to keep from dying of hunger: after all, everyone's got to live. But when one side completely outwits the other, they find nothing better to do than to make themselves at home, and suck the delicate fat which covers my ribs: I'm used to it. An irritable viper has eaten my penis, and taken its place: that bitch has turned me into a eunuch. If only I could have used my paralyzed arms to defend myself; but I think they've changed into logs. Anyway, it's important to notice that blood no longer spreads its rosy coloring over them. Two small hedgehogs whose growth has been stunted, threw the inside of my testicles to a dog, which didn't refuse: carefully washing out the skin, they crawled inside. My anus has been intercepted by a crab; it stands guard at the entryway, encouraged by my inertia, and hurts me a lot! Two jellyfish came across the sea, quickly tempted by hope which was not disappointed. They looked carefully at the two fleshy parts which form the human behind. Grappling onto their convex exterior, the jellyfish applied such a continuous, crushing pressure that the two hunks of flesh disappeared, leaving behind two monsters, emerged from the viscous realm, equal in color, form and savagery. Don't talk about my spinal column, because it's now a sword. Yes, yes . . . I wasn't paying attention . . . your question deserves an answer. You want to know how it came to be planted vertically in my back, right? The fact is, I don't really know; nonetheless, if I decide to take for a memory what may only be a dream, know that man, when he learned of my vow to live with sickness and immobility until I had vanquished the Creator, came walking behind me on tiptoe, but not so quietly that I didn't hear him. For a brief instant, everything went blank. This sharp knife plunged in to the hilt between the shoulders of the fighting bull, and his bones shuddered like an earthquake. The blade was so powerfully stuck into the body, that no one has been able to draw it out. Athletes, mechanics, philosophers, doctors, they've tried all kinds of methods. They didn't know that the harm man has done cannot be undone! I pardoned the depth of their native ignorance, and blinked my eyes in greeting. . . .

(Canto IV, pp. 264-266.)

* * * * * *

The intermittent destruction of human faculties: whatever your opinion may be, those are not just words; at least, not like other words. Let the man raise his hand, who thinks he will perform an act of justice by asking some executioner to skin him alive. Let the man lift his head with a voluptuous smile, who would willingly bare his chest to the bullets of death. My eyes will look for the scars; my ten fingers will concentrate all their attention as they carefully explore the flesh of that eccentric; I will check to see if any bits of brain have splattered onto my satiny face. Do you really think anyone could be found in the entire universe, who wanted to be martyrized in that way? It's true, I don't know what laughter feels like, never having experienced it myself. But it would be reckless to claim that my lips would not extend, if I ever encountered anyone asserting that somewhere such a man existed. What no man could possibly desire for his own existence has unjustly befallen me. Not that my body swims in the lake of pain; no, it's not that. But my mind is scorched by a condensed, always active reflectiveness; it howls like frogs in a swamp, when a flock of hungry herons and flamingos settle in the reeds along its bank. Happy is the man who sleeps peacefully in a bed of feathers plucked from the eider breast, without knowing how he has betrayed himself. For more than thirty years I have not slept. Since the unspeakable day of my birth, I have sworn eternal hatred to the boards of sleep. I myself wanted it that way; there's no need to accuse anyone. Quick, get rid of that aborted suspicion. Can you see this pale crown on my head? It was tressed there by the skinny fingers of tenacity. As long as the hot sap runs in my bones, like a flow of molten metal, I will not sleep. Each night I force my livid eyes to stare through my window at the stars. For more security, I prop my swollen eyelids apart with wooden splinters. When dawn appears, it finds me unmoved, my body still vertical and upright against the cold plaster wall. Sometimes I dream, but without for an instant losing the strong sense of my personality, and the ability to move about freely. You should know something else too: the nightmare which hides in the phosphorescent angles of darkness, the fever exploring my face with its stump of an arm, each awful beast that lifts its bloody claw, well, it's my own will

that makes them move around me, giving nourishment to its
tireless activity. . . .   *(Canto V, pp. 294-296.)*

* * * * * *

"Every night at the hour of deepest sleep, a huge old spider
pokes its head slowly out of a hole in a corner of the room near
the floor. It listens carefully to hear if any noise still waves its
mandibles in the air. Being an insect, it cannot help but attribute
mandibles to the noise, if it hopes to increase the riches of
literature with a few brilliant personifications. When it is sure
there is only silence in the room, the spider, unaided by meditation, withdraws the various parts of its body from the nest, and
advances carefully toward my bed. Now this is strange! Although
I can force sleep and nightmare to keep their distance, I feel my
whole body paralyzed while the spider climbs up the ebony foot
of my bed. It holds my throat in its claws, and begins to suck my
blood with its belly. What do you think of that? How many
quarts of a purplish liquid whose name you know, has it drunk
since it started this routine, with a persistence worthy of a better
cause? I don't know what I've done to provoke this action. Did I
inadvertently step on its leg? Or steal its little ones? These two
rather doubtful hypotheses don't hold up under serious scrutiny;
they easily cause me to shrug my shoulders and to smile ironically, although it's wrong to mock anyone. Careful, black tarantula; if what you're doing doesn't have an irrefutable syllogism
for excuse, one night I'm going to spring awake with a last gasp
of my agonizing will, and break the charm you've used to keep
my limbs paralyzed. I'll crush you between the bones of my
fingers, like a lump of something soft and sticky. And yet, I
vaguely remember having given you permission to climb onto the
swell of my chest, and from there to the skin which covers my
face; therefore, I haven't the right to stop you. Oh, who will help
me to straighten out my confused memory? I'll give him the rest
of my blood as a reward; including the last drop, there's at least
enough for half an orgy cup." He talks, while undressing. With
one leg on the mattress, and the other supported by the sapphire

floor, he maneuvers himself into a horizontal position. He has resolved not to close his eyes and to await his enemy. But doesn't he make the same resolution every time, and isn't it always undermined by the inexplicable image of his fatal promise? He is silent now, and painfully resigned; for him a word given is sacred. He wraps the silken folds around him majestically, and scorns to knot the gold buttons of his curtain. Resting his wavy black hair on the fringes of a velvet cushion, with his hand he explores the large wound in his neck, into which the spider habitually crawls as into a second nest; his face breathes contentment. He hopes this very night (hope with him) will see the final enacting of the great suction; because his deepest wish is for the executioner to end his existence: death, and he will be happy. Look at that huge old spider slowly poking its head out of a hole in the corner of the room near the floor. We aren't in the story anymore. It listens carefully to hear if any noise still waves its mandibles in the air. Alas! we are in reality now, as far as the tarantula is concerned, and although I could put an exclamation point at the end of each sentence, that is perhaps not sufficient reason not to do so! Now the spider is sure there is only silence in the room. See it withdraw the various parts of its body, one after another, from the depths of its nest, unaided by meditation. The spider stops for a minute; but the instant of hesitation is short. It says to itself: the time has not come to stop torturing, first it must give the condemned man some plausible reason to explain the perpetuity of his torment. It has climbed close to the sleeper's ear. If you don't want to miss a single word of what the spider is going to say, eliminate all the foreign preoccupations that block up the gateway to your mind, and at least be grateful for the interest I'm showing in you, by allowing your presence to attend these theatrical scenes which seem to me worthy of exciting real attention on your part; because, what would prevent me from keeping the events I'm talking about to myself? "Wake up, amorous flame of the old days, dried out skeleton. The time has come to stop the hand of justice. We won't make you wait long for the explanation you desire. You're listening to me, aren't you? Stop moving around, you're still under our magnetic power,

and the encephalic atony remains: it's for the last time. What
impression does Elsseneur's face make in your imagination?
You've forgotten it! And Reginald with his bold manner, are his
features engraved in your brain? Look at him hidden in the
curtain folds. His mouth leans close to your face, but he doesn't
dare speak to you, because he's more timid than I am. I'm going
to tell you the story of an episode in your youth that will help
you along the road to memory. . . ." Some time ago, the spider
had split open its belly, and two boys had rushed out of it,
dressed in blue; each of them held a flaming sword in his hand,
and now they stood beside the bed, as if to stand guard over the
sanctuary of sleep. "This one hasn't taken his eyes off you,
because he loved you very much and was the first of us to whom
you gave your love. But your stormy character often caused him
pain. He tried his best not to provoke you: an angel wouldn't
have succeeded. You asked him one day if he wanted to go
swimming with you in the ocean. You leapt together from a high
rock, like two swans; hands clasped, arms extended before you,
you slipped through the aqueous mass, like skilled divers. For
several minutes you swam under water, coming to the surface at
a great distance from shore, your hair mingled together and
soaked with the salty liquid. But what mystery had occurred
beneath the waters, to cause a long trace of blood to be seen on
the waves? Once on the surface, you went on swimming, pretended not to see the growing weakness of your companion. He
rapidly lost his strength, but you kept on stroking powerfully
toward the misty horizon, which disappeared before you. Reginald cried out in distress, but you pretended not to hear. Three
times he echoed out the syllables of your name, and three times
you answered with a voluptuous cry. He was too far from the
shore to go back now, so he tried vainly to follow in your wake,
hoping to catch you and rest his hand for a moment on your
shoulder. The negative chase went on for an hour, he losing his
strength, you feeling yours increase. Finally, in despair of equal-
ing your speed, he prayed briefly to God to spare his soul, turned
over on his back and floated; we could see his heart beating
violently in his chest. In that position he awaited death, so as not
to wait any longer. By that time, your vigorous limbs were out of

sight, and were getting further away all the time, like a sinker
you let go of. A fishing boat suddenly appeared, after having
placed its nets further out at sea. The fishermen thought Reginald was a shipwrecked sailor, and they hauled him into the boat,
unconscious. They noticed a wound in his right side; each of the
experienced sailors expressed the opinion that no pointed reef or
rock fragment could have pierced a hole so microscopic, and yet
so deep. Only some cutting weapon, like the sharpest of all
stilettos, could claim the paternity of such a subtle wound. He
never wanted to say what happened during that long dive underwater, until now he has kept the secret. Tears flow now over his
pale cheeks, and fall onto the sheets: memory is sometimes more
bitter than the thing itself. As for me, I will feel no pity: that
would show too much respect for you. Don't roll those furious
eyes in their sockets, keep calm. You know you can't move.
Besides, I haven't finished my story.–Lift up your sword, Reginald, don't be so quick to forget your revenge. Who knows?
Maybe one day it will come to accuse you.–Later you felt a
fleeting moment of remorse; you decided to compensate for your
error, by taking another friend. By such expiation, you hoped to
wipe out the soiled past and give to your second victim the
friendship you hadn't been able to give to the other. It was a vain
hope; character doesn't change from one day to the next, and
your will remained what it had been. That is when Elsseneur saw
you for the first time, and from that moment I couldn't forget
you. We looked at each other for a minute, and you began to
smile. I lowered my eyes, because I could see in yours a super-
natural flame. I wondered if you had fallen secretly among us,
one obscure night, from the surface of a star. Now that there is
no need to pretend, I will confess, you didn't resemble the wild
boars of humanity; a halo of gleaming rays enveloped your head.
I would have liked to become intimate with you; but I was afraid
to approach the overwhelming strangeness of your nobility; a
feeling of stubborn terror crept around me. Why didn't I listen to
those warnings from my conscience? Warnings that were only too
well founded. Noticing my hesitation, you blushed too, and held
out your arm. I bravely put my hand in yours, and that made me
feel stronger; from then on, a breath of your intelligence had

entered into me. Hair blown by the wind, breathing in the wild surges of the air, we walked straight before us for a while, through groves thick with lentisk and jasmine, with pomegranate and orange trees; their perfumes overwhelmed us. A savage boar brushed by us at full speed, and a tear fell from his eye when he saw me with you. I didn't understand what he was trying to tell me. By nightfall we reached the gateway to a big city. The silhouette of domes, minaret spires, the marble globes of belvederes stood out clearly against the deep blue of the sky. But you didn't want to stop and rest in that place, although we were terribly exhausted. We walked around the outer fortifications, like nocturnal jackals, avoiding the watchmen; finally we reached the road on the opposite side, and left behind us that solemn gathering of reasonable animals, civilized as the beavers. The flight of lamp-carrying birds, the hiss of dry grass, the intermittent howling of a wolf in the distance, accompanied our obscure and hesitant way through the countryside. What good reason did you have to shun the hives of man? I asked myself that question, a little uneasily; besides, my legs were beginning to weaken after such prolonged effort. At last we reached the edge of a thick wood; its trees were laced together by an inextricable network of vines, parasitical plants, and cactus with monstrous spines. You stopped near a birch tree. You told me to get down on my knees, and prepare to die; you gave me a quarter of an hour before I had to leave this earth. I remembered some fleeting glances you had directed toward me during our journey, when you thought I wasn't looking; some movements whose irregularity I had noticed. Suddenly they were like an open book. My suspicions were confirmed. I was too weak to resist. You threw me onto the ground, like a hurricane tearing at a willow leaf. You put your knee on my chest, and the other knee on the wet grass; one hand grasped both my arms, and I saw the other pull a knife out of a sheath suspended from your belt. Unable to resist, I closed my eyes: the rumbling of a herd of cattle was heard in the distance, carried by the wind. Prodded by the shepherd's stick and the jaws of a dog, the herd advanced like a locomotive. You saw there was no time to lose; you were afraid you wouldn't be able to do what you had planned, because the approach of unexpected help had redoubled my strength. Seeing that you could only hold one arm still at a time, you settled for a quick movement of the blade, cutting off my right hand at the wrist. The neatly detached piece fell to the ground. You ran off, and I fainted from the pain. I won't tell you how the shepherd helped me, nor how long it took for me to recover. Let me simply say that your unexpected betrayal made me want to give up living. I sought out wars, and exposed my body to the risks of combat. I won glory on the field of battle; my name caused even the bravest men to tremble, as my iron hand wrought bloodshed and destruction in the enemy ranks. Then one day, while cannon shots thundered more loudly than usual, and whole squadrons were torn from their sockets and whirled around like straw by the cyclone of death, a horseman approached boldly, challenging me for the palm of victory. The two armies stopped and watched us in silence. We fought for a long time, covered with wounds, our helmets shattered. Then we agreed to stop for a while and rest, before beginning again with renewed strength. Full of admiration for the other, each of us lifted up his vizor: "Elsseneur!...." "Reginald!..." Those were the words our panting throats pronounced together. Reginald had fallen into a bottomless despair; like me, he had entered the career of arms, and the bullets had spared him. What a way to meet again! But your name was not pronounced! He and I swore eternal friendship, different, to be sure, from those two earlier friendships in which you had been the principal party! An archangel came down from heaven with a message from the Lord, ordering us to change ourselves into one spider and come each night to suck the blood from your throat, until a command came from on high ordering us to stop the punishment. For almost ten years we have haunted your bed. From today on, you are delivered from our persecution. That vague promise you spoke of was not made to us, but to Him who is more powerful than you are: you understood that it was better to accept this irrevocable decree. Wake up, Maldoror! The magnetic charm which has weighed on your cerebrospinal system for so many long nights is dissolving." He woke up as he had been commanded, and saw two heavenly forms vanish in the air, arm in arm. He did not try to go back to sleep. One by one, he displaces his limbs from the bed, and goes to warm his icy skin at the embers of the Gothic fireplace. He is wearing only a shirt. With his eyes, he looks for the crystal pitcher, to moisten his dry mouth. Opening the window, leaning on the sill, he looks up at the moon which pours over him its cone of ecstatic rays, filled with silvery, palpitating atoms, like night moths, ineffably sweet. He waits for the dawn with its change of scenery, to bring a paltry comfort to his shattered heart.   *(Canto V. pp. 312-320.)*